making it

To my family who loved and lived with an unconventional woman

making it

What I Got Away With
in Hollywood

REBA MERRILL

RARE BIRD | LOS ANGELES, CALIF.

Rare Bird Books
453 South Spring Street, Suite 302
Los Angeles, CA 90013
rarebirdlit.com

FIRST TRADE PAPERBACK ORIGINAL EDITION

Set in Minion
Printed in the United States

10 9 8 7 6 5 4 3 2 1

Library of Congress Cataloging-in-Publication Data

Names: Merrill, Reba, author, interviewer.
Title: Making It: What I Got Away with in Hollywood / by Reba Merrill.
Description: Los Angeles, CA : Rare Bird Books, [2021]
Identifiers: LCCN 2020013413 | ISBN 9781644282359 (paperback)
Subjects: LCSH: Merrill, Reba. | Actors—United States—Interviews. |
Motion picture producers and directors—United States—Interviews. |
Motion picture industry—California—Los Angeles. | Motion picture
journalists—United States—Biography.
Classification: LCC PN2285 .M47 2020 | DDC 791.4302/8092273 [B]—dc23
LC record available at https://lccn.loc.gov/2020013413

FOREWORD

I can remember the first moment I met Reba Merrill. She had a certain style and manner you don't often encounter in this business, a seductiveness that was purely business but totally enchanting.

Reba made me feel like I was the most important person in the world, at least at that moment. Again, I will use the word seductive. I was working as a producer at Entertainment Tonight and she was doing electronic press kits for studios or EPKs as they are known. Usually, this kind of homogenized canned movie star interview was handed off to me by studio publicists. Generally, I ignored the interview portions because they were so promotional in nature I could hardly make compelling television out of them. Anyway, we did our OWN interviews. But not always. The rare exception was almost always a Reba interview.

There was something uniquely different about her work. It actually was watchable. Unlike most of these studio-sanctioned interviews she managed to cut to the chase and get to the heart of her interview subjects whether it was a big star or some third level supporting player. I am still not sure how she did it, but I think I developed some of my own interviewing style just watching her stuff on those tapes. She had the knack, but I was surprised she ever got hired to do these because the material was so NOT what I had come to expect from these manufactured interview packages. Reba knew how to sell a movie precisely by not selling it and she got remarkable insights from all those many stars, some of them certifiable legends. Somehow, she used those seductive powers to get what she wanted and you could just tell that after a long day of press they were glad to see her.

Reading her remarkable story of how she found her groove in this business you come to realize the makings of a real pro. She suffered the slings and arrows of what was expected, all those years in local TV, struggling to get ahead, to find her path, her rhythm and her self-esteem. It wasn't easy. And it clearly was tough navigating the shark-infested waters of show business—but she did it. And continues to do it in her own inimitable Reba style. And now she's written this highly entertaining memoir and, as usual, pulls no punches. Read it. Enjoy it. Be seduced by it.

Pete Hammond
February 12, 2021

Pete Hammond is a writer, producer, movie critic and film historian. His analysis and commentary on the entertainment industry has appeared in print, on air and online for numerous publications including *The New York Times, Los Angeles Times, USA Today, Entertainment Weekly, New York Magazine, OK Magazine, NBC Nightly News with Tom Brokaw, Evening News with Brian Williams* on MSNBC, CBC, BBC, Bravo, E!, and AMC.

1
UNPACKING THE DREAMS!

I'm not a writer. I am a talker, in fact, I talked this book into my computer with the help of Dragonspeak. If I hadn't been able to talk and talk and talk, I would never have had a career in the entertainment industry. I would never have been able to figure out how to travel the hills and valleys, actually, the mountains of life.

Looking back on my life, I must have been crazy to think that I could start over again in, of all places, Hollywood. But then again, I knew at five that I wanted to be a performer. I can clearly remember standing on the white steps of our neighbor's Baltimore row house singing my heart out for our neighborhood talent show. I sang "A-Tisket, A-Tasket," not bad for a tot who could neither carry a tune nor tap dance, but that didn't stop me from performing.

When I got married, years later I thought it was forever because he was everything my mother wanted for me. He came from a wealthy family, the right religion and well educated. I worked in local television and was even the face of Continental Airlines on TV in 1960. For me I could not handle the "Mad Men" of advertising who thought my paycheck included other perks for them.

My television career ended after the sixth Continental Airlines commercial. After eight years of marriage, my husband walked out on me and our two daughters, ages three and five.

I will never forget moving from my Country Club lifestyle into a basement apartment on the other side of the railroad tracks. I was scared for my future. I knew I had to find a husband because my Mother made me believe I was only good for marriage. I dated a lot of men in my search for a husband. Many men wanted me, but the ones I wanted were not interested in a destitute, divorced woman with children. Life took hold of the wheel and I packed my dreams away and never thought I would get a chance to recapture them.

Finally, I met the man who not only loved me but also my daughters, Diana and Cheryl. He encouraged me to go back to college and that's when my life began to change.

Let's face it, being a model or a PR person for a glass company didn't exactly accomplish anything except to put food on the table for my children. All though I added a multitude of jobs from charm schoolteacher, fashion coordinator and a commercial spokeswoman. I had no thoughts of a full-time career until I got a television show.

After following my husband's job moves—which took me to Sacramento; Washington, DC; London; and Los Angeles—I ended up in Phoenix, Arizona. In every place we lived, I did TV commercials or voiceovers, so I was starting to unpack my dreams.

My television career really started when we moved to Phoenix, Arizona. I have to be honest, I really hated Phoenix. I didn't like the weather or the house, but my family was happy. My children loved being in school and my husband loved his job, so I was the only one who was miserable.

In Phoenix I appeared in a commercial and hated it. Even though I had appeared in other commercials, I thought saying the words for that particular product made me sound stupid. I came home and announced to my family that instead of doing commercials, I would get a talk show. After the laughter subsided, I had to figure out how to actually do it. I looked up Phoenix television stations in the phonebook; there were only five at that time. Before I started on this adventure—and I have never told this to anyone—I created a "vision board," pictures of the things I wanted to happen to me. I cut out the call letters of the five Phoenix TV stations from TV Guide, and then out of other magazines I cut five TV sets. On each screen, I placed a picture of myself. Then I called all five stations and got appointments with executives at each one. I wish I could remember what I said to get in. Whatever it was, it worked, as I got into each station, but after my meetings, everybody turned me down.

I had a perfect record, no one wanted me!

If I had any hope of getting a television show it was when I met Burton LaDow, the general manager at KTVK Channel 3, then the ABC affiliate in Phoenix. He said, "not yet," a powerful response that gave me hope because I knew what "yet" meant: the difference between yes and no. All I had to do was get rid of that "t" in yet and I had a "yes."

I hosted a TV show for a non-profit organization at the TV station. After the show I went to see Mr. LaDow and asked him what he thought. He said he hadn't seen it. As I drove home, I was crushed because I knew the show was good. It was fun, it was light, I got the message out, and dealt with the ups and downs of the production. I handled everything that happened in that show with ease and I was devastated to find out that the man who might hire me didn't even watch it. That show was my audition tape.

I was home for about an hour and the phone rang. It was LaDow's secretary, who said that he would like to talk to me. "You're not bad. I saw it, I had it taped." Then he said, "You are not bad, but not yet." There again was that "yet." I was getting discouraged because I knew I could host my own show or at least thought I knew I could, and yet it was still a "not yet."

I had another meeting at channel 3 only this time the eighty-year-old owner who was the former governor of Arizona was there. After questioning me for close to an hour, he said "Burton, give her a show!" The show called Reba was born.

In reality, the reason I was hired was not that the governor recommended me, but the National Organization for Women was going to picket the station because it did not have any women on the air.

I had a television show for four weeks at twenty-five dollars a show. Finally, I was doing what I wanted to do. I was always aware of who was coming to Phoenix for a lecture or a gallery showing. About a month before I went on the air, I went to Burton LaDow and said, "This very famous lady is coming to town. I really would like to interview her while she's here and then run it as one of the shows." He said okay, so a week before I really went on the air (we already had the set) I interviewed Françoise Gilot who was in town for a retrospective of her artwork. I had bought her book to read about her life. My first question was, "You have lived with two of the most famous men of the twentieth century. You were Pablo Picasso's mistress and had two children with him, and now you are Dr. Jonas Salk's wife. Being French, does that make you great in the kitchen?"

I knew the answer, because I'd read the book and knew that cooking wasn't her skill. She burst out laughing and said to me, "It wasn't cooking—there were other places where I really excelled." I was watching Burton out of the corner of my eye and he was having a really good time.

So, I did my first interview. I knew it was good, and it taught me a lesson. I knew all the answers to the questions I would ask. After I got through with the taping, Mr. LaDow came to me and said he thought I should stay for eight weeks. Needless to say, I stayed a lot longer (over two years) and I learned a lot on their nickel, or, in this case, their twenty-five dollars.

On the fourth show I got to interview veteran newsman Hugh Downs, who had moved to Carefree, Arizona, a Phoenix suburb. He was still working in New York, so he would come out to Carefree on weekends. One time when he was there on vacation, he came to the studio on a Wednesday afternoon for a live show. I had researched all of his books and had my clipboard with a list of incredible questions, but during the interview I realized I was more concerned about my questions and was not listening to his answers. I went to a commercial, and when we came back from the break, I put the clipboard down and said, "Mr. Downs, you have earned a living in radio and television interviewing. Will you teach me?"

We spent the last half of the show with him giving me advice and me listening. Because I had no clipboard to depend on, I just had a conversation with a very famous interviewer. I absorbed as much as I could. Months later, when I interviewed his wife, Ruth Downs, a knitting expert, Hugh joined her. After the interview he said, "Do you know how many people ask for advice?"

I said, "Well, I guess a lot."

"Do you know how many people follow the advice?" he asked, "I have no idea," I replied.

He said, "Very few, and you were one of the few. You are turning into a very good interviewer."

By now, I had doubled my salary to fifty dollars a show and within another three months I was up to seventy-five. After a year, I was making one hundred dollars a week at the TV station, I was giving speeches, and I was really, really happy. I was also learning, polishing, and finding out how far I could push myself, as well as how far I could push my guests.

Phoenix was a convention city that drew lots of famous people, which gave me a wide variety of celebrity guests. I will never forget the interview I did with world-famous psychic Peter Hurkos. His forte was called psychometry, which was the ability to see past, present, and future by association with an object that he touched. He saw pictures in his mind like a television screen when he touched an object, and then would describe what he saw. This fascinated me.

After the show was over, he asked me if I wanted a reading. Never one to turn down a free anything, I jumped at the chance. I gave him a ring I wore every day; it was made from the stones I got from my failed first marriage, but to me it represented my renewal. After a few moments he looked me in the eyes and told me I was going to have a very successful career, different from what I was doing now. Sounded intriguing, and I was thrilled. What did I have to lose? I got my first television show by using a vision board, so now I'll use a psychic. I was willing to try anything as I loved having a career, something I never thought would happen to me.

The summer after I got let go from KTVK, I went to New York and, because I had worked for ABC, I decided I wanted to meet with Bob Shanks, the creator of *Good Morning America*, probably one of the greatest programmers at the time.

One advantage of being a big shot at the ABC network was that your office was on a very high floor. I got on an elevator to the fifty-sixth floor. The only other person on the elevator asked me where I was going. I said, "I'm on my way to meet with Bob Shanks. I used to work for ABC in Phoenix and I want to see what kind of options are open to me."

I went in, had the meeting, and got him to autograph his book, but left without another job. I was so naïve that I had thought that since I came from a local ABC station, doors would open for me to work at the network.

When I was leaving the building, I ran into the man from the elevator again, and he invited me to lunch. Over lunch he asked, "What are you going to do now?"

I said, "I don't know. I have a week in New York that my husband treated me to."

He said, "Well, it just so happens that HBO is looking for an interviewer to do a presentation on cable, which is to be given to the Lionel Van Deerlin Congressional Committee on Cable Regulations."

So this man, whose name I can't even remember, took me to meet with Russell Karp, president of TelePrompTer Corporation, Gerald Levin, president of HBO who eventually became the chairman of Time Warner, and Steve Elliot from Screen Gems. These were the men who were going to decide who would conduct the interviews. They talked to me and gave me the job. I didn't have to do anything for the production except the actual interviews, and they set those up for me. I interviewed cable subscribers, actors, and producers, and even the flamboyant film director, Otto Preminger. They put me up at a hotel, paid all my expenses, and actually paid me for the six weeks I spent in New York City doing the interviews.

At the time, I didn't realize how important cable television was going to be. HBO, which is now one of the largest and most prestigious cable networks, offered me a job doing interstitial pieces, interviews to be played between movies. Coincidentally, that is where my celebrity interviews would air a decade later. In 1976, cable television was just getting started, and I wasn't impressed that HBO had offered me a job. At that time, HBO was just playing a lot of movies; they didn't have any original programming. I didn't take the job because it would have been impossible for me to work in New York and commute back to where my family lived in Paradise Valley, Arizona.

When I returned from the high of my trip to New York, I was so depressed that I just sat on the floor all day. A very good friend of mine, artist Agnesa Udinotti, saw how down I was and offered to take me on a trip. "I'm going to California, I have things I want to do [more romantic than business-related], and I'll drop you off in LA" she said.

There had been an agent in LA who had contacted me to talk about representation. The talk show world is a small one. He had heard about me, but at the time he called I still had my show in Phoenix and never considered leaving. I had no idea that he was a very influential agent.

When I decided to go to LA, I set up an appointment with Noel Rubaloff the agent. I arrived at his office, which was very, very large and had a huge desk. Across the room was a leather couch and an end table with a phone. He asked, "Well, what have you been doing?"

I said, "Nothing, but I want to get another television show." "How can you get another TV show if you have not done anything about it?" he asked.

"Well, I still have one tape out at KFMB, CBS in San Diego."

He then wrote me a script, dialed the number, gave me the phone and told me to say exactly what was written on that script. The call was to Jules Moreland, the program director at the CBS station in San Diego at that time. "I'm going to be in San Diego in a couple of days. Do you think I could stop by and say hello?" I read.

When he said yes, I suggested, "Is there any chance we could have lunch?"

He said, "Absolutely not."

I replied, "That's okay, I'll be there." I flew down to San Diego only to see him. I got there about 11 o'clock. The station was not that far from the airport. I went in and met with him. We started talking, and the time just flew by. He said, "Come on, let's go grab a bite." So, we had lunch, and afterwards, as we were walking back, he said to me, "I want you to come into the studio and I want you to interview me." I had no time to prepare or do any research; all I knew was that he was the Program Director.

I decided to base my interview on the responsibility of television when it comes to violence. It was a very long interview, and at the end all he said was, "Thank you very much. By the way, you're in the finals. We are making a decision and will call you on Monday." This was the same station to which I had sent my demo tapes two months ago, so they must have been interviewing applicants for quite a while.

I flew back to LA and then home. When Monday came, I sat by the phone all day. They didn't call. Ever since my return from New York the conversation around the dinner table was all about HBO. We talked about how exciting it had been and how thrilled I was to have been offered a job working for this new cable network. We talked about it so much that you would have thought I was going to take the job.

On Tuesday, after the CBS station failed to call, I went out and ran all the errands that I didn't get to do on Monday. I was out when they did call and our eleven-year-old son Mark answered the phone. They said that it was KFMB calling from San Diego about the possibility of a television show. My son replied, "I don't think she's interested, she's had an offer from New York." Out of the mouths of babes! I could not have said that myself. When I finally got back and he gave me the message, I called back and they said, "We'd like you to come out tomorrow."

I said, "I'm terribly sorry, I can't be there until Thursday." Their response was, "Fine."

The reason I didn't want to go out the next day was that I wanted to get my hair done, make sure I had the right dress, practice my makeup, and make the best impression possible.

I arrived at the San Diego TV station on Thursday afternoon. They asked if I would interview one of their reporters.

I was cool and comfortable. Little did I know that the interview was being viewed by as many women as they could find, many of whom were the wives of the executives at the television station, as well as other women who worked there. That afternoon they offered me a position on *Sunup San Diego*. I had been approved by the co-host, Mel Knoepp, who acted as if he liked me because when we sat on the couch together, I appeared much shorter. I have very long legs and a short body, so when we had to stand up together, I had to take off my shoes. When they offered me the show, I called my husband to share the exciting news and he said, "You can't do it," to which I replied, "You don't own me."

When they offered me the job, they asked me two questions: what was I earning and what was my age? I was so embarrassed about the amount I was earning in Phoenix ($125 a week) that I tripled it, but I told the truth about my age, which was the first big mistake I ever made in my career. On television it didn't matter how good I was or that the viewers loved me—all they could see was my age. Even though I was forty-one, I beat out everyone else, especially the young women just out of college.

I finally had the challenge of doing an hour TV show, five days a week, which was brand new for me. It was an interesting, exciting and scary time, but deep down I really loved it.

2

HARRISON FORD

This was a perfect solution to continue my career and keep my marriage in-tact. I remember thinking this psychic really knows what he was talking about because my daily show in Phoenix was small potatoes compared to the show I just got offered in San Diego. I loved the show, the city and the people I met. I didn't love my cohost who considered himself Mr. San Diego, but in reality, he was the real Ron Burgundy right down to his polyester suits. The *SUNUP* show gave me the polish and the opportunity to interview some amazing movie stars. I was charmed by Ann Baxter, who was in my most favorite film, *All About Eve*, Peter Finch for the film *Network*, and Harrison Ford in *Star Wars*. I was a local star. I could draw a crowd at a grocery store opening or sell raffle tickets at a charity affair.

Reba: One of the most exciting young men to hit the motion picture industry in a long time, Harrison Ford, and you will be seeing him as a superhero in *Star Wars*. That's if you're willing to stand in line. Do you realize what's happening with that movie?

Harrison Ford: Yeah, they keep telling me.

Reba: You have to well, let's see, I think a strong back, comfortable shoes, a lot of food…

Harrison Ford: Oh, don't go any further than that, that's a well-known cliche.

Reba: What? Tell me.

Harrison Ford: The one about comfortable shoes. Never mind. Go on.

Reba: This is a morning program so you have to be careful. Did you realize that *Star Wars* was going to take off like that?

Harrison Ford: No. I mean I was aware of the fact that we were making a movie that was accessible to everyone, that it was going to be fun, but I don't think anybody could have predicted the success that we're now enjoying.

Reba: I was wondering what Harrison Ford is really like.

Harrison Ford: This is it.

Reba: I know this is it.

Harrison Ford: Except that I'm nicely dressed.

Reba: But the thing is that you started an acting career and then you stopped.

Harrison Ford: Yeah, started about thirteen years ago and I did the first three or years of my career on a contract with Colombia Pictures. I freelanced a little bit. And then I really wasn't getting anywhere with my career. I was stuck pretty much in the same place where I started.

Reba: Which kind of place? As a pretty, young man?

Harrison Ford: Not as a pretty young man, I kept playing the same part over and over again, the guy that didn't do it, the guy with a scene at the beginning of the show where they said, "We've got your rates and you did it," and then they come back in the middle and then they say, "Well, we're not so sure. Would you tell us your story again?" And then there's a scene at the end where they come in and they say, "You didn't do it?" And I said, "I told you that at the beginning, but I understand you guys were just doing your job." But I really didn't like that.

Reba: Wait a minute, it takes guts to take and pull out of something that you probably really loved in the first place to get into, like being an actor.

Harrison Ford: Yeah.

Reba: And just completely put it out of your life, at least for the time being. You went into the carpentry?

Harrison Ford: Yeah.

Reba: What were you going through? What were your feelings and your thoughts to do something like that?

Harrison Ford: Well, I started when I was twenty-one years old. I was a baby actor. I was a baby person at that age. I'm a little bit of a late bloomer, I guess. And I wasn't ready for the inevitable rejection that you have to face.

Reba: Oh, it does hurt. Tell them how it hurts.

Harrison Ford: Well, it's hurts, and so I took some time off to regroup, to learn to do something else, to invest my energy in something which I could really... The worst part of it was not being able to work hard enough, not having enough work, not having enough of something to concentrate on.

Reba: The thing about the starving actor is really true?

Harrison Ford: Oh, it's all true.

Reba: Did you make any money as a carpenter?

Harrison Ford: Reba, how could you ask me a question like that? Actually, I made more money as a carpenter than I ever had as an actor, sure. I have a wife and two kids, and I was glad to have the opportunity to do that.

Reba: What was it like raising children in the film colony? I was just talking to Carrie Fisher and of course she came from superstar type of environment, which doesn't really exist today. I think Hollywood is a lot more realistic about their actors. I mean you are a consummated craftsman.

Harrison Ford: A craftsman, at least. Well, I don't know, we live a very quiet, private life. We don't have a whole lot of social life.

Reba: Are you going to shelter your children?

Harrison Ford: Shelter them?

Reba: Keep them out of the public eye.

Harrison Ford: No, I shouldn't think... Well, I don't think people should be sheltered, as such. I don't think that they should be denied access to reality, but my kids are pretty level heads on their shoulders.

Reba: Have they seen the film?

Harrison Ford: Yes, they have.

Reba: Are they impressed with their father?

Harrison Ford: They love the movie. I'm not sure that they... I don't know what goes on in a kid's mind when they see...

Reba: One of the things been missing from television, from the film industry has been a hero that young children—and I say the word children—could identify with, and I think you and Mark have given two clean cut heroes for young people to identify with.

Harrison Ford: Right.

Reba: I mean, I have an eleven-year-old and he didn't move. And it's not a short film. The film was over two hours. And I haven't been to a film in a long time where people applauded at the end. That's what was so amazing. Maybe it was because they were so glad they had a seat.

Harrison Ford: No, I mean, George is a wonderful filmmaker and he's created a film that not only children enjoyed. I went to Grauman's or the Chinese Theater here in Hollywood about three days ago to see it for the first time with an audience.

Reba: You didn't have to stand in line, did you?

Harrison Ford: No, I did not. But I did look at the line as I went in and there were very few kids in it. It was eight o'clock at night on a Wednesday night, but the line was composed pretty much of young people, middle-aged people, old people—not a lot of kids. I have this feeling that parents were taking the opportunity to see this film before they let their kids go, not because they wanted to judge it for themselves but because they really wanted to see it.

Reba: And then they get to see it twice.

Harrison Ford: Yeah, and then they get to see it twice.

Reba: Harrison. Do they call you Harrison?

Harrison Ford: Yes.

Reba: The whole formal…? Look at that, I said your name and you really blossomed.

Harrison Ford: Yes.

Reba: You're not going to drop out again, are you?

Harrison Ford: I hope not. I have my tools packed and ready.

Reba: Your carpenter tools?

Harrison Ford: Yes.

Reba: Actually, I think it means something else. It was kind of a very beautiful expression "your tools packed and ready." I think it describes you; you have everything kind of together now. You're definitely star material, and I don't mean to say that embarrassingly, but this time if you would drop out, I think a lot of people would be unhappy, not just you.

Harrison Ford: That's very kind of you to say so.

Reba: So, I hope that you've got future plans. I hear there might be a sequel to what we just went through.

Harrison Ford: Yeah, and we hope to start the sequel in a year.

Reba: Anything else on the horizon? Are you superstitious?

Harrison Ford: No.

Reba: If you had something cooking, would you say it?

Harrison Ford: If I had signed, I'd say.

Reba: Do you have anything cooking?

Harrison Ford: I have a lot of things cooking and nothing signed.

Reba: But you're not afraid this time, are you?

Harrison Ford: No

Reba: Do you think you'll be typecast?

Harrison Ford: No.

Reba: I don't know what to say, I don't know if anybody is aware of this, but you have the most devastating green eyes, it's not easy to talk to this morning so I think I better just leave.

Harrison Ford: You're very kind. Nice seeing you again, Reba.

Reba: It was nice seeing you. We've been talking to Harrison Ford of *Star Wars* and we'll be back after these messages.

◆◆◆

For some reason this is the only interview that survived from my morning TV show. I remember I was a nervous wreck at my first junket. I was not surrounded by the comfort of my set and more importantly I had done no prior research. Normally I do quite a bit before a guest came on my show. Instead, I relied on the studio production notes, to work with which was a big mistake.

Everything was shot on film with a mag sound strip, so when I returned to San Diego, I gave my director the film cans which he transferred to tape and gave me the cans back. I put them in a shopping bag and forgot about them. When I moved to LA I found the bag which only had one film can and no label so I was really surprised that the film can had an interview of Harrison Ford and the bigger surprise was that it survived. This interview was never seen again after it played on my CBS show.

When I sat down with Harrison he was warm and charming. Later, when Carrie Fisher's memoir, *The Princess Diaries*, came out in 2016 she wrote, his "potent pot" caused her to forget a lot of the details from that time. Portions of her book were taken from notebooks she located renovating her home. She gave Harrison Ford the final galley of her book and he signed off on it. Maybe that's why he was so charming, and I always wondered if that's what he used to get over being painfully shy and awkward. I guess this piece of history which I have protected for so many years was meant to survive. I tried for a year to sell this interview to George Lucas's company for their archives but in true Hollywood fashion they gave me the run around and finally would not return my calls. You will be able to see this interview at the new Academy of Motion Picture Arts and Sciences museum. Just ask to see it.

3
HOLLYWOOD REALITY

I loved working on television doing a morning show. It came to an end when I was fired by CBS, which I thought could be for my age—I was in my mid-forties—and then received seventeen rejections from other TV stations. Which brings me back to the psychic: if I truly believed he was right—that there was something bigger out there for me—I had to think of ways I could use my skill as an interviewer and hide my age all at the same time. I thought I would go to Los Angeles and try to get a job interviewing off camera. Even though I knew how Hollywood felt about women of a certain age, I was prepared to lie. I felt I had nothing to lose. I made up my mind to try one more time. For most of my married life, my husband, Jan, had always challenged me to do things. He provided a secure home base for me to venture forth fearlessly knowing I always had a safe place to return.

His belief in me was what had enabled me to get into television in the first place.

This changed when I told him I wanted to look for work in LA. My husband thought this was foolishness and would not support it. I had done four local television shows and won an Emmy; what more could I possibly want in my career? I have no idea where the courage came from that pushed me to go to Los Angeles and find a job without my husband's financial support. But I did.

With no financial help, I needed a place to sleep, and I turned to Milton Rich, a press agent from New York, who had done publicity for my CBS show. He knew a famous casting director in Los Angeles, Barbara Claman, who was willing to let me stay on her pullout couch in exchange for doing errands. In between I could look for work and figure out my future.

Milton Rich also got me a meeting with a division president at a major film studio, who was beginning to produce electronic publicity marketing materials. I was so excited for this meeting. My heart was pounding as I walked into his office. When I sat down, he smiled and said, "Not only is your work good, but you look like you came from central casting." During that meeting he showed me how he set up shooting on film sets, how many days were needed, what they were sending out to local stations, and how they delivered their publicity materials. I took this all in and was flattered when he said that he could find a lot of work for me and asked me to join him for dinner to discuss the details.

He chose a fancy restaurant in Beverly Hills, expensive and delicious. He wanted to discuss how I would fit in and what would be expected of me when producing these publicity materials. I was getting more excited as the meal progressed, and then came dessert. He promptly let me know that I could have all the work I could handle, and the only thing I had to do was go down on him three times a week. To be honest, I thought it was a joke. This was the first time in my life, especially my professional life, that such a crude and blunt offer had been made to me for a job. When he called me a week later to ask if I wanted to work at the studio, I knew this was code for sex, and the answer was "no." However, this was not an easy answer to give, as I was desperate to work.

That was the career I dreamed of and here it was served to me on a silver platter; however, the price was too high. My choice led to me being blackballed from that studio for eight years. The one good thing to come from that meeting, and the most important, was I had learned how to promote films by using video interviews and behind- the-scenes footage from film sets. I knew that I could replicate and improve on their methods by using my background working in local television. In fact, I knew what I needed to do.

I would create a television network made up of local stations not invited to the press junkets—which I had done for CBS by offering them an exclusive finished profile. The studios were sending too much material that would cost the local station time and money to put a programing segment together; I would solve the problem with just a movie-star interview. This video profile was a complete package that allowed the on-air anchor to replace my voice and introduce the segment. It gave local stations a Hollywood connection and I could hide my age. It was a win-win proposition.

I told Milton Rich about the real offer his contact at the studio had made and asked for help to create a TV network. Rich was also a consultant to 20th Century Fox and was able to get me a room with a telephone and a book that listed all US television stations. I had the room for five days and called television stations and asked news directors the following question: "Will you take canned material from Hollywood?" If the answer was no, I went on to the next station in the same city, until I got a yes. Then, I said, "I will be your Hollywood producer. Tell me what you want." Every station said, no matter which city, "We will take the hype if you humanize it."

Creating the TV network turned out to be easier than I had anticipated because I knew there were only a set number of journalists on a video press junket. By the end of the week, I had fifty-five television stations willing to play my interviews.

My first opportunity to use my network came with a call from Doubleday Books with an offer to shoot an interview with Irving Wallace for his latest release, *The Almighty*. Much to my surprise, they ran his video profile and that really confirmed I had something. Now that I had my network, I was sure the studios would see the value I would add to their films and hire me. What I wasn't prepared for was that not one studio would take my calls. I didn't know how the Hollywood game was played, and I wanted to learn how to play it, so I needed to get help.

I knew what I had would be valuable if I could just get to the right person, so I started networking. I would go to any industry event, talk to everybody, and finally at an event I got a suggestion to call anybody I knew that worked at a studio for the marketing division.

Funny it had not occurred to me to reach out to an old acquaintance, Chris Arnold, who had his own company, Cimarron, producing trailers for Warner Bros. I had worked with him when I was at CBS and we stayed in touch. The advantage of being an attractive woman was that I was comfortable enough to call him and suggest lunch, knowing he would pick up the check, which was important as money was tight. I told him about the fifty-five stations that had committed to run my interviews and that all I needed was a contact at a studio—and that if he would help me, I would give him fifty percent. He agreed, and, like a fairytale, he actually got a movie three weeks later from Warner Bros. called *Cujo*.

The movie was ready to be released, so all I was able to do was an interview with the star, Dee Wallace. I knew I needed more than just scenes from the movie to make the segment appealing to the stations, so I had my video crew shoot footage of her home with her husband, the film posters hanging on her walls, and her personal scrapbook.

I sent my first movie star profile out in July 1983, weeks before the film opened across the country, and waited for the reaction. I soon heard from the stations: they loved it. The morning shows used all of it, the news shows cut the profile in half and ran it for three days—two days of the profile and one day with a review. I had created a winner. Then came the money from Warner Bros., and my partnership with Arnold ended when he took ninety percent and I took the master and left. My first big lesson: get it in writing. But I'm glad now that I didn't have a written contract because what I created was a sensation;

I knew I had a winner, and it was all mine.

4
ROBERT REDFORD AND PAUL NEWMAN

I knew I was on the right career path when my *Cujo* project had shown me that it was just a matter of getting to the right person. But getting to the right person required some luck. In my networking around town, I was introduced to Arthur Canton, a retired publicist who was willing to help me because it gave him something to do. He called Andy Kean, who was the president of Kaleidoscope, which was one of the most successful Hollywood trailer companies at the time. When I met with Andy Kean, I never mentioned a partnership, but I did say I could run a division for him. I showed him my station list and the response cards from my Dee Wallace movie profile. I definitely dazzled him. He said, "I have one more day of shooting behind the scenes on the film set of *The Natural* with Robert Redford for a one-hour special I am producing for ABC. Come and ask your questions for your three-minute television profile segment."

I had never been on a film set and there I was in August of 1983, meeting Robert Redford, so I thought I'd better dress for the occasion. I wore high heel boots and a silk dress. I didn't realize that a film set has concrete floors and was very dusty and dirty, so by the time I sat down with Redford my feet hurt, and I was a wrinkled mess with a headache, but the adrenaline took over and I loved it. He went to the University of Colorado with a baseball scholarship but was kicked out for heavy drinking. I asked him which drinking establishment he liked, Tologies or The Sink. He laughed, and the ice was broken.

Later I found out he worked and drank at The Sink and his face is prominently portrayed on the bar's mural to this day. Since

Andy Kean kept the original interview, here are a few sound bites from the produced profile.

Reba: What does this film mean to you?

Robert Redford: I think my doing the film has something to do with fathers and sons. I think it could probably be said that a lot of this has to do with this being for my dad. He used to play ball with me. In fact, one of the most wonderful memories I have of my dad and me in any kind of a connection was talking while we played catch. He would come home from work and I would wait for him and I would have the ball in the mitt and I would say, "Will ya toss the ball with me?" and he would, and I didn't realize at the time that it was a form of relaxation. He could put the war out of his mind, he could put the work out of his mind, whatever was bothering him, and he could throw the ball back and forth with me so there's a nice rhythm to that and we would also talk. It was also free of any kind of rancor or any kind of expectations; "Why are you failing at school?" "Why did the principal call your mother into the office?" "Where were you last night after dark?"—none of that. We would just play ball and talk so I appreciated that.

Reba: Your first career choice was not acting but art.

Robert Redford: I thought it was important to come up with something that sounded real when people said "what are you going to do when you grow up?" or "what are you going to be?" that I come up with something that sounded solid like art direction, which sounded really solid but I didn't know what it meant. I said it just so people would say, "Well, that sounds good. Art direction. Solid. Whew. I thought he was going to be an artist. This is much better." So, I would have the hounds away from the door for a couple of years and in that state, I got into acting kind of by accident, but the truth is, I wanted to be an artist. I just was either ashamed, embarrassed, guilty—probably guilty, too guilty to say it, but that's what I wanted.

After my Redford interview, Andy Kean told me that he felt I would be perfect to work on his next project promoting *Harry & Son* and sent me to Malibu to interview Paul Newman. I knew that my strength came from doing a lot of research before I sat down to interview anybody, especially superstars. Since this was before the internet, I relied on the best place in town to do all the research; it was the motion picture academy library and all it cost me was twenty- five cents for a locker. I could Xerox some of the greatest articles ever written about Hollywood stars for just twenty-five cents a page. I had a field day reading all about Paul Newman before I went to Malibu.

The film *Harry & Son* starred Newman and his wife, Joanne Woodward, so it gave me a chance to ask the star—and the director—what it was like to work with his personal leading lady. Joanne served us refreshments before the shoot and really made me and my crew feel comfortable.

Reba: What is the best thing about acting?

Paul Newman: I like all of the preliminary work, I don't know that I actually like standing in front of a camera and if my work has been done well, it's been done before we ever turn a foot of film.

Reba: Did the role of Harry bring back memories of the relationship with your own father?

Paul Newman: My father died before I had made the professional decision to continue with acting as a career, so I don't know whether we would have had that battle or not. There's no one who will go to the movie and not be able to recognize something of the conflict that goes on in the family. The difficult moment, for me as an actor, when I look at the kid and know I can't take him anymore. Movie stars are supposed to be able to take everybody in all these situations and to find the bewilderment and the discomfort and it was an interesting moment for me to play that person.

Reba: How is it to direct your wife?

Paul Newman: It can be difficult. It can be easy depending upon the scene, how far she's along in terms of her development. But always rewarding. I mean, if it were too easy, there wouldn't be any fun connected with it and there wouldn't be any challenge connected with it. I know when to keep my mouth shut with her and to give her a chance to do it differently than I would want her to do it or to even make a mistake and to give her a free shot at it is what I'm trying to say. And, a lot of time, she just blows my socks off.

Reba: What make your marriage successful?

Paul Newman: I think the marriage is successful because we listen. A lot. And because I don't mean to give the impression that this all been cherry pie and ice cream. Stormy, difficult, impossible, insensitive, but never boring.

Reba: Why car racing?

Paul Newman: Joanne has an interesting theory—she thinks that one of the reasons I started racing is that I was just getting really bored with acting and she thinks that some of the passion for racing has bled back into my acting and that I got charged up again. I can't comment on that, but I think the lady knows me better than I know myself.

I knew before I sat down with him that he hated the film *The Silver Chalice*, his first film, and even tried to buy all the prints so no one could see his performance. What did surprise me was an article by the famous Hollywood gossip columnist Hedda Hopper, who saw *The Silver Chalice* and wrote all about Newman, and ended the column declaring he was Hollywood's newest star. After the interview was over, I told Paul Newman about the Hedda Hopper column. He asked to see it, and after he read it, asked, "Can I keep this?" I realized that was the best twenty-five cents I had ever spent, and in that moment, I felt very important.

I realize how surreal this was. First, I couldn't get anybody to give me the time of day and then within a short span of time I was able to sit down with Robert Redford and Paul Newman. I was so amazed I had to pinch myself. The original raw interviews are gone but I was able to find these moments from the produced profiles. It was a miracle that they survived as tape usually doesn't last over thirty years. Another lesson learned: keep the masters.

5

JACK LEMMON

I learned a lot working for Andy Kean. He taught me about the business of Hollywood, and, in reality, he taught me how to make money in Hollywood. He told me to look at my interview as a hunk of baloney and to sell it by the slice—if they want more, you charge them all over again. I did that with a straight face and it really worked. He also taught me to be very careful whom I talked to about what I was doing because people in Hollywood have been known to take an idea and use it as their own. The biggest thing he taught me was how important contacts were. I did three movies for Andy: *The Natural, Harry & Son,* and *Stick* with Burt Reynolds. Each was a delightful learning experience.

When I was not working on any of Andy's projects, I spent my time networking, and that's when I met Bill Shields, president of marketing at New World Pictures. A week later, I got a call from him about producing interviews to publicize *The Philadelphia Experiment.* He was not only pleased with how I turned the footage around, but also realized how valuable my television network was for distributing publicity materials for independent films. I walked away from Kaleidoscope and struck out on my own when New World Pictures agreed to be my first client. I knew I would get more work this way, I just didn't know what, where, or when. Before that took off, I met the woman who would change my career forever.

I had known of Michele Reese, vice president for publicity at Universal Pictures, for a long time but couldn't figure out a way to meet her. I met a man from a smaller company, Avco Embassy Pictures, whose name I cannot remember, who had worked with her, and he told me if I took him to lunch he would introduce me. He picked the Palm Restaurant and proceeded to run up a very hefty bill. When I went to reach for the check, he took it and said that had been a test and he would set up the meeting.

I walked into Michele Reese's office and the first thing she said to me was, "You don't remember me, do you? I was on your television show in San Diego and never forgot how good you were to me." Vice presidents of studios don't take meetings with unknowns, but obviously I wasn't.

Once we started talking, I could see she was intrigued. I showed her my station list and the comment response cards from the *Cujo* profile I had sent out. I was a little concerned to tell her that a lot of the stations paned the film in their reviews. I thought it would blow my chance at getting any work, but all she asked was if the stations were really using the video profiles and I said here's my list, call anyone you want. She must have believed me because she gave me my first major studio job. Michele Reese taught me the biggest lesson about what was important to the studio marketing division: get the movie clips played. Movie clips and more movie clips played even if they came with not-so-great reviews. It's in line with that old Hollywood adage: it doesn't matter what they say as long as they say my name.

Before she gave me my first project, she made sure I knew that she was sticking her neck out for me at Universal and that if I failed, I should have the decency not to come back. I had enough faith in my abilities and knew that I was not going to fail. My assignment was to produce a profile on Jack Lemmon that showed clips from the movie without talking about the film too much. The movie was Mass Appeal, which dealt with the relationship between the Catholic church and homosexuality. She told me how much she had budgeted for this project, and it was more money than I had made for a year working at CBS. With a straight face I told her I would make this work. Then I went to my car and screamed.

It was my job to sell the movie, though I really wanted to do an Oprah type interview and forget about the other part. But I had to pay the piper or none of this would exist. The biggest challenge I faced was to do an interview that sold the movie but had the feel of a more intimate conversation. The secret was to open the video package with a personal story. Usually it had to do with something from their childhood or from the beginning of their career or a funny story that happened on the way to getting famous. Everything I did had to be approved by the studio, sometimes even by the star, and of course their publicist. I walked a very fine line trying to please everybody when I really only cared to please the local station producers of shows that were willing to play these promotional interviews. Timing was everything. The stations had to receive a three-quarter inch tape at least a week, two at the most, before the film opened in their city. They would promote that the star would be on their show and usually did that for a few days before the interview ran.

I knew this was my big chance. Not a bad start to sit down with an icon like Jack Lemmon. In 1984, there was no behind-the-scenes footage, so everything I was going to use in my profile I had to create. I was given the telephone number for Jack Lemmon and was told by someone on his staff what day he would do the interview at his office. I countered, "I don't want to do the interview at his office. I want to do this interview at his home; that's what my viewers want to see." I forgot that I was interviewing him for a celebrity publicity profile, and I didn't have any viewers as I didn't have a talk show. They agreed to let us go to his house in Beverly Hills for the interview.

It was an unbelievable experience. He was the most charming man I had ever met. He graciously opened his home to us and gave us hours of his time. There I was sitting with a two-time Oscar winner.

He let me shoot his walls, which were filled with amazing studio stills, including color pictures from the black-and-white film *Some Like It Hot*. In the picture, Jack wore a pink outfit while Tony Curtis wore blue. I also shot his baby book, the Hirschfeld drawings, and commercial advertising photos. When it came to my questions, I loved the exchange as nothing was off-limits, and I knew he was comfortable from the way he reacted. I had always been interested in finding out what made celebrities tick and here was my chance. He even sat down at the piano and played music that was his own composition as I explained we didn't have money to pay for music.

Reba: Are you flawed?

Jack Lemmon: Sure, I'm flawed; we all are. You do two things, I think, in living: first of all, you try to overcome faults as you recognize them in yourself, and after your family and everyone else tells you twenty- four hours a day for about thirty years that something's wrong, you begin to believe them. And you adapt certain characteristics that you may not like about yourself, and you try to temper them to change and also to live with yourself and respect yourself.

Reba: Does a role ever frighten you?

Jack Lemmon: Oh, yes. This is crazy, Lemmon's Law, when you get a really good part, there's a little fear for me, and then I don't want to turn it down for fear that I'd be turning it down and rationalizing that, "Oh, it doesn't interest me," when basically it's that I'm afraid I might not be able to do it, and you do better work when you're a little afraid. I truly believe no matter how fortunate, how talented, whatever happens, nothing on God's green earth that is truly worthwhile will be easy—nothing, because if it did come easy it would not have the same impact, but that makes it all the better.

Reba: Have you ever brought a character home?

Jack Lemmon: The worst experience I had about bringing a character home was—and you never know why it will happen. Days of Wine And Roses was a deep drama about a raving alcoholic, and that didn't affect me as much as Save The Tiger, which was about a guy having a nervous breakdown and going through a tug of moral war within himself about whether or not to set his factory on fire during a bad economic year and collect the money for it. I began to have the same symptoms and I would come home and I'd be having dinner, literally one night, and I just started to cry and I started to shake and I started to sob, and I knew what it was, thank

God, but I couldn't stop it. And it was very close and you get to that dangerous ground where the character takes over the actor. That's no good. The actor must always be in control. It should seem to an audience that it is the character, but the actor has to be in control, but sometimes it does happen.

Reba: When did you know you wanted to act?

Jack Lemmon: I wanted to be an actor from the time I was approximately nine years old. I was in a school play and the costume was too big and I looked silly and didn't know my lines, so they started laughing every time I said something. I could have been terribly embarrassed, I guess, because I really was kind of shy and I wanted desperately to be accepted. And instead of being embarrassed, something went off in my mind that "I think I like this." They were paying attention and they were laughing.

Reba: First break?

Jack Lemmon: Television was just burgeoning, it was just opening up, you know, the old days of black and white; it was all live, there was no tape, no film, but primarily there were no stars. So once you got a foot in a door, which in my case was a couple of years before I could at least earn a living, which is really not very long, but it was due primarily to the early days of television. And I must've done 500 or 600 shows in about six years or so. So, it really was a marvelous training.

Reba: What would you have done if you had not become an actor?

Jack Lemmon: If I hadn't become an actor, and I have thought about this, I don't know what I would have done because it's the only thing that I've ever done, it's the one love that I wanted, plus it worked. Even in the bad times, in the first few years where I would doubt myself, I had the faith always and did not lose it but there's got to be some self-doubt in there or you're not human. I don't know what I would have done because there has never been a point where I really thought, "Well, if this doesn't work, I'll try that." Fortunately,

I still to this day don't know what I would do if I didn't do acting.

Reba: Have you ever failed?

Jack Lemmon: Oh, yes. One of the worst things about being an actor or a politician or anybody that is in the limelight, in the public eye who is a known quantity, your failures are picked up immediately. Not only do you have to deal with critics, but they will really lambast you, and millions of people read these reviews-"Lemmon is a lemon," whatever it may say. However, you can also be lauded. But have I failed countless times? I don't know anybody who has had a durable career, and I have had over thirty years in film and theater, who has not failed.

Reba: Do you care what people think?

Jack Lemmon: I would be crazy if I said I didn't care, and yet, it's peculiar, I do care, but never would I try to create an image purposefully just to be liked or to be acceptable or Mr. Nice Guy or this and that. I would not do that.

Nothing in the world that is worthwhile that has a point of view is going to please one hundred percent of the people. I do want to be respected above all. I would rather be respected than liked, if that makes sense. And I don't want to try to appeal to the broadest number of people, as an actor or as Jack Lemmon. Of course, I want to be liked, but above all, I would rather be respected.

Reba: Do you take risks?

Jack Lemmon: Do I take risks? It may not seem that way to someone who sees my films. As a result, if you are lucky, and I have been, and you get a very good film, you're going to try to keep that level up. You have to read an awful lot of scripts before even taking one. And the only way I'm going to get that excited is to try to find something that I don't think is close to what I've done and that maybe I can pull it off; it's a risk and I have to be afraid. If you're afraid to risk, you lose.

Reba: People identify with you as drinking too much?

Jack Lemmon: Well, it is true. I still get mail from a film that's twenty years old, Days of Wine and Roses. At the time I did it, the public identified me with the part I played. I got a tremendous of amount of mail from very intelligent people that believed the film to such an extent that I became the character; in their mind they were trying to tell me how to quit drinking. I think it's very difficult to play a drunk, and that's one of the reasons why I loved that film because it worked. I'll tell you the truth, playing a drunk is very tricky. Well, if you drink and try to play a drunk you can stay there for weeks, you're never going to get one take, the actor will lose control. Playing it is a different thing.

For me, personally, I'll tell you, I just quit drinking because I found it too compulsive, I could not handle it, and I certainly didn't want it to affect my work or my personal life. Also, being older, my body isn't quite what it was, and I find that anything with alcohol will tend to upset my stomach so that's a part of it. But I feel a little better about it. I don't want to worry about something, and I certainly don't want to lose control of something. I guess it's just ego or whatever.

Reba: Do you tell white lies?

Jack Lemmon: If it's important I would not dream of doing it, but I will admit I do. I think we all do it, probably. I'm not saying it's right again, but we do it. I would much rather not hurt somebody if I can help it and I hope they won't hurt me if they can help it, you know, if it's not all that important.

Reba: What personal commitments have you made?

Jack Lemmon: The personal commitments that I have made to myself is how to be remembered. I want the highest level of respect that I can get. The only time I have been disappointed more than public rejection or critical rejection of my work is my own rejection. Now, that may seem self-serving, but it's something I think that's very important. We think of success in this country too often being based on how much money you made or what some other idiot thinks of you. That is what it is. I think it certainly should be your own opinion of yourself and then hopefully, God willing, others might have a high opinion. But most important is a high opinion of yourself for yourself. And that is the thing that I have strived for most of my life.

Reba: Tell me about *Some like It Hot.*

Jack Lemmon: When we started Some Like It Hot and realized that for eighty percent of the film I was going to be running around in drag with high heels, dresses, wigs, and makeup, and I wondered if some people were going to say, what is he, a swish, or is he a fairy, a transvestite, or whatever? The first time I put on the full makeup with the wig and the dress I really was shocked, and I was worried. I said, "Are we going to get away with this?" I was nervous and I was scared about it. The only thing that made me feel good was Tony Curtis, who was right beside me in all of his get-up, got a crazy idea, and said, "All right, let's test it," and he grabbed my hand and marched me into the nearest ladies' room. We walked in where the girls check their makeup and we fudged around with lipstick and stuff and combed our hair. At least fifty girls that were working on other pictures walked in and out of the ladies' room and never batted an eye. Someone said, "Hello, honey, what picture you are on?" And we said, "We're doing a new film." And we did it and nobody batted an eyeball, and I said, "We're in." I've loved Tony ever since.

Reba: Did you always play the piano?

Jack Lemmon: I took lessons for a few months when I was eight or something like that, and as much as I love music it just did not take to then. And fortunately, my parents did not push it. When I was thirteen or fourteen going away to boarding school, I suddenly fell in love with music and wanted to do it, and I couldn't take lessons then, so I just started doing it by ear, and it's been great. I kind of miss the fact that I can't read music, but by the same token it's a great source of satisfaction for me to sit and learn by making mistakes and everything. I can play for an hour and think it's five minutes.

Reba: What's the secret of your successful marriage?

Jack Lemmon: First of all, my wife's patient. Patience keeps this marriage going. But ultimately, I never knew what love was, really. I didn't know I had that capacity, and that's one of the reasons; it was too much to lose. It has been enriched not because of me or a great deal because of her, but because of us. And there is a tremendous attraction that has never diminished there but there is one other thing that I never did before that she makes me do and made me do and made me realize I shouldn't feel so guilty about letting everything out. There's no holding back or bottling up, and I used to do that because I was worried about what people might think of me or how I was supposed to be behave. We fight like you don't believe, and it's one of the reasons it's a terrific marriage because there's nothing holding it down. And we have a fight we don't then spend the next two weeks thinking, My God, the marriage is going to hell. It's good for a marriage, it's more honest and so forth.

Reba: What is life-like now?

Jack Lemmon: I'm fifty-nine, but I feel now ten years younger than I did ten years ago. And I don't know what it is except there's a certain peace of mind I have. At the moment, I am very content personally and emotionally with my family and with my career. I don't feel as uptight as I used to be, I don't worry about the long waiting for the next terrific part. I'm more grateful for the ones I've already had. As I got into my early fifties, I think that I probably was saying, "You're getting very old, you haven't seen to satisfy anything that you really wanted to do. I wonder if you're going to be able to fulfill yourself as much before you get to be old." I don't have those fears.

Reba: Any regrets?

Jack Lemmon: Not major regrets in my life or in my profession because I had to finally grow up to realize, "Hey, you're going to make mistakes and you're going to make a lot of them." The wonderful thing is that when I have made mistakes, wrong choices of material, bad performance, whatever it may be, it certainly wasn't intentional and it's going to happen. It's been so counterbalanced with the highs and the ones that really did work. And Lord knows in my personal life, whatever mistakes I've made—a failed marriage in the beginning, which certainly was my fault if anybody's. But no, I think that probably I have learned as much or more from mistakes I have made in my life than I have from successes.

Reba: Do you believe in luck?

Jack Lemmon: In other words, does luck play a part in your life? I think that there is a great deal to be said for any actor, no matter how talented—and probably in any position in life—no matter how hard he works, there is no guarantee of success or even making a living, of making a dent. I am convinced that there is God-knows-how-many actors walking up and down the street out there that could have played any of those parts that I was lucky enough to get. I was at the right time in the right place, and someone opened a few doors for me, and it's got to be very important. But, by the same token, when they close the door behind you, you have to deal with it. So, I don't feel guilty about it. I feel that I've had an excess of it. But yes, I have been helped at times. For instance, I did a test as an eighty-year-old man—in fact, you couldn't even recognize me under the makeup which disguised me. John Ford happened to see that test. It had nothing to do with him , but his next picture, which was going to be Mr. Roberts. When he saw the test by mistake, he said, "Who is that?" and somebody said, "Well, that's a new young kid that's under contract here at Columbia." And he said, "Really? Well, I'll tell you, I never saw a worse old man, but God, he'd make a good Pulver," and I got the part. Now you tell me that's not luck. Luck is very important.

Reba: What keeps you contemporary?

Jack Lemmon: A love of life. One thing that I have noticed as I have lived, the people that really excite me are the ones who have never lost the capacity for excitement and adventure. And we can talk about a sense of humor or the ability to love, but I think it was the capacity for excitement. And it's astounding how many people lose it, the light goes out. They've lost interest, they are depressed, everything gets to them. If we lose the capacity of hope, excitement, and interest, the quest to find out about life and things going on around us, then we have lost the reason to live. We exist; we don't live.

◆◆◆

The day ended with him telling me how much he enjoyed our time together. I asked him if he really meant it and he told me yes, so I asked if he would put it in a note and he agreed. I don't know where I got the courage to ask as I had never ever asked for anything from anybody before. I had brought my daughter Cheryl, who was visiting from San Diego, and I now believe Jack Lemmon's enthusiasm came from her very short romper outfit and her great legs. The interview with Jack Lemmon made me aware that I was not scared but definitely excited, and I knew that this was where I belonged. Was I really going to have my dreams come true?

Once the studio saw the note, I was elevated to a trusted in- demand-video producer of publicity materials. I saw Jack Lemmon one more time in 1996 when I was doing the video publicity for Getting Away with Murder that he starred in with Lily Tomlin. I said, "I don't know if you remember me, I interviewed you for the movie Mass Appeal and you sent me this amazing note. Would you like to read it?" He answered, "You read it." I couldn't get through it without crying. I said, "I don't know how to thank you for putting my career on the fast track." I never saw him again. Jack Lemmon passed away from bladder cancer in 2001 at the age of seventy-six, but his legacy and my memory of a generous man live on.

JACK LEMMON

August 14, 1984

Dear Reba,

I just wanted to drop you a line and tell you
how much I truly enjoyed doing our tape session the
other day.

Having been in this crazy business for three
decades now, I hate to think of how many interviews
of this type I have been involved with in the past,
but I can honestly tell you that I have seldom enjoyed
one as much as I did ours. First of all, you're bright,
you're stimulating, and you really do your home work.
Your questions are intelligent and incisive, and I never
once felt, "Oh God, here we go with that question again
for the 100th time!"

In short, although I don't know how long the session
lasted, I could have kept on going with no qualms whatsoever. And believe me, that's not the usual reaction!

Again, my many thanks for making something that is
usually work a genuine pleasure.

Please give my very best wishes to your delightful
daughter and save some for yourself.

And may the wind at your back never be your own!

Always,

Jack

Ms. Reba Merrill
645 Westmount Drive
Suite 212
Los Angeles, California   90069

6
CHER

I no sooner finished the Lemmon interview when I got my first job to shoot on a film set. Lucky for me *The Boys Next Door* from New World, starring teenage Charlie Sheen and Maxwell Caulfield, was a small independent one. This film taught me a lot as I had to build a budget, hire a video crew that had worked on a film set before, and plan a timeline. It gave me a chance to learn what was needed as I had never been in charge of shooting behind-the-scenes footage and on-set interviews. I must admit that I did not know what I was doing, so I had to trust my cameraman, who had shot on film sets before. I realized I would need additional help and hired my daughter, Cheryl, to supervise the video crew and interact with the publicist and director. It was an excellent fit. I trusted her implicitly and she understood what I needed as had she sat in on all the editing of the first profiles. Cheryl became my eyes and ears on the set while gathering the footage needed. Then, when the timing was right, determined by the shooting schedule, I would come to the set and conduct the interviews. Sadly, none of that footage has survived.

I realized that my original concept of just delivering profile interviews had taken a big turn, and I had to be prepared to deliver a lot more than ever before. I was lucky I got into the field early because, I believe, my distribution was what really got me the jobs. I was thrilled that my television network was now up to 120 stations in just a few months. I owe that to those early profiles with Paul Newman, Dee Wallace, and Jack Lemmon.

Mask was my second film for Universal. I was told to do the interview in a photographer's studio where Cher was being photographed for the cover of *Us Weekly* magazine. Universal was very high on this film, but Cher was unhappy with the director and had refused to do any publicity. The studio promised that we would only do profiles of her costars stars Sam Elliot and Eric Stoltz and nothing on the director, and she finally agreed. I was surprised when I met her because she had cut off all her hair and had a blonde streak straight down the center like a skunk, which was a far departure from her normal look.

There was no behind-the-scenes footage from *Mask*, but we could use some of the photo stills from the film. Again, I would have to create interesting footage to enhance Cher's profile. In *Mask*, Cher plays a freewheeling biker woman on drugs who fights to get her bright-but-deformed son the education she feels he deserves.

Reba: How much of you is in your character?

Cher: She's the kind of a woman that I like to portray, a woman that's more close to what I think most people are. I'll tell you something, it's a lot easier to expose your feelings in a working situation than just to go around exposing your feelings because, first of all, it's my emotion. I don't feel that people know who I am at all, and I could give interviews from now until a week from ever and no one would ever know me because I'm very private and the way I stay private is being very public. I feel like I can answer anybody's questions and yet nobody really knows me and that's kind of the way I'd like to keep it.

Reba: Is there anything that you can't do?

Cher: I only do a couple of things well and so acting is kind of the thing I think I can do best. I'm not a great singer. I'm not really a great dancer. I'm pretty funny, but I think acting is what I do best.

Reba: I don't think people realize that—how much you wanted to be an actress—and I didn't get the feeling that the acting community wanted you.

Cher: No, they didn't. When Sonny and I started doing the TV show, it was really fabulous to be able to do those sketches and we had a really good time doing them and we did them for a long time, and then I wanted to do something more. And a perfect and honest example of what people thought was I went to Joe Papp and he said, "How do I know if you're talented from all that shit you did on TV?" So that kind of really made me angry and also determined at the same time. And I said, "Fine, you give me something to do. I'll come back here and do it and audition for you." And he did. And I went back to do the audition for him. And that was the day when I came out of the audition, I went back into his office and there was a message that I should call Robert Altman, and I went to see Robert and he gave me the script and said, "Read it." And that was on the weekend. And then on Tuesday, he said, "Well, you're right. You should play Sissy and the parts yours."

Reba: Do you get nervous?

Cher: The last time I was really nervous to do a show was when I did The Phil Donahue Show and I was terrified. I don't usually have those kinds of nerves anymore because I've done it so much. But that really scared me. I was going to sit in front of 250 women who were going to have to like me in spite of the fact that I cannot remain constant and remain looking like someone who's likable or someone that's ordinary or whatever. And what I went in was a black leather jacket, the short black skirt, and this hair. But it scares me a lot that it's like I want to really be liked. And yet I'm still rebellious enough to have to have it on my own terms. But I think I really am a good person for women to like, because I really believe in the strength that women have, and I don't feel that I'm like this feminist, but I much prefer the qualities that women have.

Reba: How was the experience?

Cher: I was terrified, but they were fabulous. They were really, really nice. And, also, I realized at that time that what I was projecting about myself was what I was actually projecting on them. I was looking at them and they looked a lot different than I did.

And they're going to ask me these really punchy questions and are not going to like me. And the fact of the matter was they were very nice, and we were all the same no matter what we look like. And that's something that I had forgotten.

Reba: I would've thought that once you got the chance to act, you would have been scared.

Cher: I was scared before I went to do *Silkwood*, I was packing my bags, and I said to my sister, "I'm not going." She said, "Why?" And I said, "Because I can't possibly work with Meryl Streep my second time. I just am not ready for it, maybe later, but not now." My sister said, "You know, they saw your work, let them be the judge of it." And once I got there, I was never nervous again except for one scene that had nothing to do with Meryl. I didn't learn my lines. I kept blowing them.

Reba: But what was it like to work with Meryl Streep?

Cher: It was like a day at the beach. I mean, it was easy. Meryl is very, very easy to work with and whatever nerves you have working with her is something you've got to bring there by yourself. I mean, she would absolutely not help you be afraid of her.

Reba: What does it feel like to be an actress?

Cher: I think it's a good job. I think it's hard, but I think that if you really want to do it, it's very rewarding. And I don't even know why, it's a stupid job, really, getting up and pretending that you're somebody else and you get a lot of money and people think you're fabulous. But there's something while you're actually doing the process that's very like going to church. It's only profound to the person who's doing it, really. And then if by some chance you can lock into something and other people will feel it, then that's when it does everything it's supposed to do, but it's a stupid job. You know, it's like not like being a surgeon.

Reba: Are you a risk taker?

Cher: I think so. It's like in this career, I don't think I've been a risk taker because when you've got nothing, you've got nothing to lose. You know? I didn't have anything. People already didn't think I was talented. They just thought I wasn't, so that all I could do is either confirm their feelings or change their minds.

Reba: How did you deal with people who don't take you seriously as an actress?

Cher: I dealt with it the way you deal with pain: in different ways at different times. I would forget about it and just think, "Okay, fine. I didn't get to be this, so I'll be this. I'll be rich." And I was doing a show most of that time, I went all over the world with this show—we did Las Vegas, we did Africa, we did every place. And then I would see someone doing something and I would think, "I could do that. I could do that if someone would just give me a chance." At the time I couldn't even get an agent who wanted to handle me for theatricals. You know, that was pretty devastating because I was the star, and I couldn't get something that a lot of people could just go in and get without even having as much exposure or have having been on the cover of *Time* magazine?

And so that was kind of devastating. I would go through periods of time where I would just decide that I would get my own property. I would cry sometimes. I would be really mean to my manager sometimes and I would be devastated. I would not care. I would be in love, I would be out of love, I would be dancing, I would be kicking up my heels in the south of France. I would be doing all kinds of different things and sometimes I would think, *Look, these people have got to be right that are running this town because if you are talented you would have already worked.*

And then two things happen. One was Francis Coppola, who I met in Las Vegas. He was scouting locations for *One from the Heart* and he came to see the show and then afterward he came backstage, and he said, "God, you are so talented. Why aren't you making movies?" And I said, "Well, because nobody thinks I'm so talented and that I should be making them." And he said, "Well, they're wrong. I don't care what anyone says, I'm right and they're wrong." And so, Francis started having me come to the studio and we started talking about things I could do and things he could develop. And it was really exciting, even though there was no work; it was enough to change my mind about things. And then I saw Linda Ronstadt onstage, and I thought, *You know, Linda and I come from the same place, I can do this.* And that's when I decided, "All right, they won't let me into movies. I'll go to New York and I'll go off Broadway." It never really occurred to me that I would go on Broadway right out of the box, but I thought, "I'll find some way to do it." And I just realized that I had to give up making $300,000 a week in Las Vegas and say, "Fine, I'm going to just forget that." And if I really want to do it, it's now or never because I don't have any more time. I don't have the years that you can take when you're twenty. I've got to either do it now or forget it, and I just made this decision that I wasn't going to forget it.

Reba: Is love important to you?

Cher: Yes, but I don't think that being in love with someone is everything to me. I don't think I'm the kind of woman who would give up everything for love. I know I'm not. I won't give up myself. But love comes in so many different ways that having some sort of love is important.

Reba: How did you manage to stay away from drugs?

Cher: I don't like them. I've tried drugs. I'm saying this from experience. It's not necessary. It just ruins everything else. I am sure that there are some people who can deal with drugs and still function in their life, but I don't believe the same about alcohol. I believe in everything in moderation, but I don't really believe in drugs at all.

Reba: Do you like to be alone?

Cher: I'm kind of a loner. I don't have many friends and I don't like to plan. If someone comes to my house, I'm really happy to see them. I never called my friends. I never call anybody back. I could stay in my bedroom for a week at a time if I wasn't going to work out, and then I go from the bedroom to the gym. It depends. I go through kind of stages.

Reba: It must have bothered you to be taken as just a song and dance girl. Did you keep those kinds of feelings inside?

Cher: Someone asked me this the other day, it was the first time I'd ever really thought about it. Had I been positive that I could do more, I would have been really, really unhappy. I wasn't sure. Had I known, had I tested it someplace and done it and known that I was capable of doing this work and not being allowed to, I would have been really crazy, but I wasn't sure myself. I wasn't sure. So it's hard to get upset, too upset, when you are not really positive.

Reba: Would you have gone back and sung and danced and performed like before?

Cher: Sure, because it was fun for me. It was an easy gig; it was something I could do well enough to get paid. I got to travel all over. It's a nice lifestyle. It's a strange lifestyle. I traveled with thirty people for three years that were like my family. And the only thing I didn't like about it was that I wasn't allowed to do anything else, and I felt, you know, no one takes this work seriously and I would like to have a chance to be able to do both, not just to do one.

Reba: Are you disciplined?

Cher: I'm so undisciplined. It's ridiculous. I am the most undisciplined person. I have a hard time completing things. I think that's why I love movies. They don't go on for a long time. You get them done and they're over with. Or television, you know, I'm working on this needlepoint; I can't finish it. I start a book; I don't finish it. I have sometimes really a hard time going to completion.

Reba: What about relationships? Any long ones besides Sonny?

Cher: No, but if you go with someone for two years—seems to be my thing—and then you break up, no one says, "Oh, it's a shame it didn't work out." If you get married and you get a divorce, they say,

"Oh, it's a shame. It only lasted two years," and this is like one of my major pitfalls.

Reba: Has fame been a disappointment to you?

Cher: I think that it was just because I was famous, but I wasn't really famous for anything except that I'd been famous for so long. I was famous just because I was famous. I really wasn't doing anything, and I wasn't really being an artist and that's really what I wanted to be. And I think that some people come by it easier or faster and some people later, whatever. For a time I felt really empty because I wasn't doing anything artistic.

Reba: Let's take it from where you are now.

Cher: I feel a lot better now about it. I feel that what I've done so far is stuff that I can stand behind and feel good about. You know, it's like I really felt good about the Sonny and Cher Show and had no idea that the powers that be took it so lightly and made so much fun of it or that it wasn't really acting. It was work and it was acting to the degree that you can do when you do an hour show, one every weekend, you've got three days to rehearse it and it's not perfect, but it was something and it just didn't occur to me that it was kind of a joke until I got away from it a little bit.

Reba: Tell me about meeting Mike Nichols.

Cher: I had gone to meet Mike Nichols for a movie called The Fortune that Jack Nicholson and Warren got me the interview on, and he just said, "No, you're not the right type." And I said, "You know, I'm very talented and you're really going to be sorry one day. I promise you that." I was really angry and yet he was being nice to me, but I didn't want that. I didn't want him to say no. I wanted him to say yes. And he came to see me on a Wednesday matinee, Jimmy Dean, and he came backstage and he said, "You know, you're really talented." I mean, he was doing it like a joke, but he had, he really remembered, and he said, "I want you to do a movie with Meryl Streep." I said, "Okay." He said, "Do you want to know about it?" And I said, "No."

I didn't believe him. I didn't think it was lying, but I didn't believe that it was going to be. I kind of thought he came to see Sandy Dennis and when he was in my room and said that, I just thought that's fabulous. And, also, this is me in a nutshell, I had just met this fabulous guy who was going to take me out between shows, and I was so excited to see him that it didn't make much difference to me because it was like, it was something over here that wasn't real. And I was excited to see John, who was real, and it was going to be there, and we were going to go out. So it kind of just, you know, it just left me. And then the next day my managers called, and they said, "You are not going to believe what's happened." And I said, "Mike Nichols wants me to do a movie with Meryl Streep." And he said, "Yes. How did you know that?" And, also, he had to get an approval from ABC Motion Pictures, who didn't want me. I mean, it was not easy. Everybody had their hardship to go through.

Reba: Does it bother you that there was a time when people considered you a joke? I hate saying it like that.

Cher: No, but it's the truth. Yes. It doesn't bother me now. It certainly bothered me then. I don't think anyone likes being taken for a joke because no matter what we think of anybody, no one's a joke. It's like a…no matter what people think of your life, and no matter how superficial it seems to the outside world or how stupid you seem, or whatever the external circumstances are, you don't feel like you're a joke. No matter if you're doing stupid things, you just don't feel like your life is a joke. It's too difficult. And I saw a television movie that Loni Anderson played Jayne Mansfield, and Jayne Mansfield always felt really badly because she was doing these things and making these choices, but she was hoping that it would lead to something else. Just the way Marilyn Monroe was hoping that it would lead to something else. And I always think like someone says, do you want to do this? And they say it will lead…you know, you'll become famous when you'll do what you want to do. And a lot of times you get stuck in this thing where you just become famous, you don't get to move on, you know? So, you have to take the chance. And at the time when you're trying to be famous, it seems like that's the only thing that's important; no matter how you have to do it, you have to do it some way.

Reba: Tell me about seeing the trailer for *Silkwood*.

Cher: We were told that the trailer was running in Westwood. So my manager and my sister and my sister's husband ran to the theater to see the trailer for *Silkwood*. And we ran in there. We were so excited. We sat down and it was a Tom Cruise movie, *All the Right Moves*, and *Silkwood* comes on.

And then it goes to Meryl Streep—black screen, white credit, and a couple of pictures of her doing different things. Kurt Russell, same, Kurt doing all kinds of things. Cher, and everybody in the audience started laughing. My sister started to cry, and I just bit my cheek and thought, "Okay, fine." I had heard from my agent that in Chicago when they had done a sneak preview of the movie, that when the credits at the top came on, everybody laughed when they said my name. And at the end when the end credits came on and they saw my name, everybody applauded. So I wasn't exactly prepared for it. But thank God Sam had told me about Chicago because I don't know how I would've felt. But no matter how I felt, it was very difficult because I had forgotten that I wasn't a movie star or even in movies as far as people were concerned because *Silkwood* was the first thing and *Silkwood* was done a year before it came out. And so lots of people in the business were starting to talk about my work, but nobody else knew about it.

Reba: Three quick questions. Do you believe in luck?

Cher: Of course. I mean, I believe in it because I'm too lucky not to believe in it.

Reba: Do you read reviews?

Cher: I didn't use to read reviews, but since the film business, I kind of have to read them. I don't believe that you should base your life on what people think about what your work is. It's like if I read a bad review of a film, it wouldn't stop me from going to see it.

Reba: And how do you handle rejection? Because now that you're in showbiz, you're not going to get every role you want.

Cher: I think I handle it okay because you can't have everything you want and not everyone's going to like you. So, I think I keep going and finally you're going to have to get something, and I think I'm pretty lucky, I get most everything I really, really want.

Reba: If you were doing this interview, if you were sitting where I am, what's the most important thing you would like the public to know about you?

Cher: I don't stop trying, but I guess there's more than one thing that I want people to know about me. It's hard to think of what it is that you want people to remember. It's like if I died on the way home and you'd have this interview, I don't know what the last thing I'd want people to know about me is. I guess that I'm a pretty okay person.

Reba: Okay. Do you have any regrets?

Cher: Yeah, but they're kind of small and I think pretty insignificant. I don't have any major ones. I think the thing that I wish I would have been able to spend more time with my kids and I think that's about the only thing that I regret, I kind of regret being married so long. I kind of wish I hadn't gotten married so early or stayed so long in.

Reba: You changed, and you speak out on things that you believe in and a lot of women are afraid to do that. Where did the courage come from to just speak your mind?

Cher: Because I figured, what's anybody going to do to me? There's absolutely nothing that people can do to you really. It's like the thing that scared me most in my life was leaving Sonny, and after I left him, nothing ever really frightened me that much again. I did the thing that scared me the most. And after you do the thing that scares you the most, there's nothing else. You know, I'm still here.

What's someone gonna do, not like me because I don't have the same opinion that they have? It doesn't bother me so much. I think people should be more vocal and honest.

Reba: You're also a lot more vulnerable than people are aware.

Cher: I don't go around showing my vulnerability that much because it's nobody's business.

Her vulnerability was as real and raw as was her willingness to take risks and reveal outcomes. Cher had no restrictions on the interview, and I felt it was a very honest conversation as nothing was off-limits. She let me shoot her private photo albums, which showed a lot of the costumes from the *Sonny and Cher Show* and the outfits from her Las Vegas appearances with millions of feathers. She did like feathers and sparkles, which I used in the profile. She also let me photograph her wigs; why she didn't wear one for the interview I will never know. This was very early in her film career, which was perhaps why she was so open with her personal stories. On my next encounter with her for the film *Faithful* she cut me to pieces as she hated everything about the film and took it out on me.

Her second film, *Silkwood*, had not been released, but would get great reviews for her. Cher told a story about being in the audience when the trailer played. She had known the trailer would be playing because she had been dating Tom Cruise at the time, and he told her the *Silkwood* trailer was attached to his film *Risky Business*.

After the interview was over, I was able to cut four different profiles, which thrilled the studio and me too as I got paid for all of them. Lessons from Andy really paid off. I sent all my video profiles featuring not only Cher's but also Sam Elliot and Eric Stolz to my stations. The profiles also played in heavy rotation on the Z channel— now a defunct cable station, but it served the areas where the majority of Oscar voters lived. Despite all the publicity, Cher did not receive an Oscar nomination for *Mask*, although she did win best actress at the Cannes Film Festival that year and received Golden Globe nomination.

The studio was so impressed with the profiles they decided to spend the money and distribute it themselves via satellite to the entire country, more than the stations I had. Universal used a national satellite company and the woman who ran it felt it was such a big deal that she immediately sent out a postcard to the who's who of Hollywood, implying she did the interview rather than just distributing the interview. I never copied anybody's work and never took credit for anybody's work and this was a very low blow. I had my lawyer Harold Lipton get in touch with her, but the damage was already done. In fact, she did a lot more damage after she got my lawyer's letter and told such effective lies to various studio executives about me that she put a dent in my career. She told them I was double-dipping, selling the interviews that the studios had paid me for. What surprised me the most was just how powerful and destructive industry gossip was and that there was no way for me to have stopped the lies. This happened nearly twenty-five years ago, yet it still goes on today.

My interview with Cher was months before my birthday, but she gave me the courage to have a birthday party even though I had already lied about my age. I realized that according to Hollywood standards I was aged out. I decided that for my next birthday I would have a big party, invite everybody from every studio, production company, and every publicist who had a star or film that I would have worked on. In fact, everybody I could think of so I would be able to celebrate with ten fewer candles on my cake. What it did was take the pressure off of aging.

I kept this charade up until I was seventy-five when my daughter insisted that soon we would be the same age if I didn't let everybody know how old I really was. The whole time I was getting all these movies I was in my fifties, my sixties, my early seventies. I got the last laugh. I didn't get aged out but sped past the Hollywood age limit.

7
JIMMY STEWART

After Cher, I didn't think anything else would blow my mind in this business, but it did when I was given the chance to sit down with Jimmy Stewart in early 1985. I was on a roll as I had gotten the chance to ask questions that turned into a conversation. I needed an ice breaker, a small start to ease my way into the interview. That would come from doing research. I knew that my best weapon was my curiosity, which dictated the kind of research I looked for. I spent two days at the motion picture library taking notes about his life and career.

I was filled with a mixture of excitement and fear, but what saved me was his publicist Paul Lindenschmidt, who was part of the velvet mafia—the underground group of gay men who had reached out to me. The personal publicist had the power to recommend work, control or stop the interview at any time. These men had power and were willing to go to bat for me when it came to my work. The eighties were the beginning of the AIDS epidemic, not only in Hollywood but worldwide. As things grew worse within the gay community, I created video profiles of some of the gay men who had helped me get a career in Hollywood. I wanted the world to know them. Unfortunately, not one of these men lived longer than two years after contracting the disease. These men were smart, talented, and very loyal, and I was lucky to have had them in my life. The video interviews I did with them have kept their stories alive so as not to be forgotten.

I was given the following directions for the Jimmy Stewart interview: only thirty minutes, I must call him Mr. Stewart, and I had to sit knee to knee because he was completely deaf in one ear and only had ten percent hearing in the other. What surprised me was that James Stewart was in his eighties and did not want to wear a hearing aid; I never imagined men were as vain as women. Following the instructions was easy. The difficult part was his cadence, which was so slow that after my allotted thirty minutes I had very few questions and answers. I thanked him for the interview and told him that I wished I had more time because there were more questions I wanted to ask. He told me to stay as long as I liked and to ask anything I wanted.

Reba: I'm sure they didn't have actors coming out of Indiana, Pennsylvania. How did your father react?

Jimmy Stewart: Not very well. When I came home and said I'm not going back to Princeton but to New York to act, he said, "Well, it's fine, you come back and take over the hardware store." My father I don't think ever really accepted it completely, my mother did. My uncle was sort of very philosophical about it, he said, "Well, there's never been an actor in the Stewart family, except one. I don't know whether to call it acting exactly but he was in the entertainment business. He ran away and joined the circus when he was a senior in high school and he ended up in jail, but that's the only Stewart that I know that was in the acting business, but I certainly wish you all the good luck and love in the world, Jim, and I'm sure everything's going to be fine." And there wasn't any reaction from anybody else, so we dropped the subject.

Reba: Did your family ever see you on Broadway?

Jimmy Stewart: They came, my mother and father came, and I think that they saw most of the plays. My mother had a lot to say about the plays. My father never said too much about the plays, but he never really talked very much about seeing me on the stage, but he still was sort of watching. And I remember he bailed me out one time when I got locked out of the hotel room. I owed them thirty-five dollars and I didn't have it, and so he wired me the sum of thirty-five dollars, but that was the only time, but he never let me forget it.

Reba: Who gave you your first movie break?

Jimmy Stewart: Well, this was fifty-two years ago in New York. I was on the stage in New York, and in those days all the big studios had New York talent scout that they would go to all the Broadway shows. And I was doing a play and the MGM talent scout saw the play and I took a test. The first test, I looked in the screen of the camera and the fella says, "Now, imagine that you see a horse, and the horse goes along the floor then it goes up and go across the ceiling and then he goes down the other wall and then he comes up to you and licks your hand." I did that and they said, "Thank you very much. Goodbye." I didn't hear anything else from them for months. And then MGM came back, and I did a little scene from the play I was appearing in as a test. About a month after that I got a call from MGM and got a stock player, a contract there. If I'd read the small print, it was a seven-year commentary, the same type of contract that was all around the movie industry at that time.

Reba: After you went to Hollywood, did you feel you made it?

Jimmy Stewart: No, that's not the way it works; it isn't the fact of getting a break and then you're home free. The more I was in the business, the more I realized that was not true. And looking back over fifty years, I don't think an actor ever stops learning. I don't think an actor can ever sort of come to a point in his life and say, "Well, here I am. I've made it." He's fooling himself if he says that because it doesn't work like that. I think you're always working to improve this idea in the movies of not having the acting show.

Reba: Describe what was the Oscar celebration like in 1941.

Jimmy Stewart: It used to be down at the Ambassador Hotel, just a sort of a get-together with everybody. It was just a wonderful evening. I still think this is what the Oscar is, just a pat on the back by your fellow workers and so on. It's a little more of it nowadays, but in those days, everybody was all dressed up and had dinner and then people would make mistakes and give Oscars to the wrong people. This was all a part of it. When I got mine, which was a complete surprise to me, I was working on a picture and I wasn't going. And somebody came to the set about four o'clock in the afternoon who was the head of publicity, he said, "I don't know where this came from, but it just came to the office that you better get home and get in your dinner jacket and get down to the Ambassador Hotel," and so I said, "All right." So, I got the Oscar, and we went out for a party after, and I got to bed.

My father never understood exactly the difference in time between the east and the west. The night after the award the phone rang at 4:30, and he said, "I heard on the radio that they gave you a prize. What was it? A plaque or a cup?" I said, "No, it's sort of a statue with my name on the bottom of it." And he said, "Well, you better send it home, and I will put it in the store window."

Reba: Tell me about Garbo.

Jimmy Stewart: I will tell it quite like I told Johnny Carson about it. I had a crush on her, but she was one of the big stars of MGM. But she was very, very shy and when she was working on a picture, the stage would be absolutely closed. When she finished work, there was a limousine at the door at a certain time and she would get in and go right from the door to the limousine and go to her dressing room, which was maybe half a block away, and then disappear. And come in very, very early in the morning. She just never came to the commissary and people just didn't see her. And I was working on the stage right next to her at one time, and I had never really seen her expect in the movies. I really thought she was wonderful. And I knew the sound man on her picture. And we were at lunch one day and I said, "Could you let me know when they break for the day and could you get me on the phone and call me when she leaves her dressing room so I can go around and see her, at least get from the door to the limousine?" He said, "Well, we'll see." One day he called, and he said, "We just broke..." He said, "As a matter of fact, I can see her now. She's just got out of the dressing room on the stage and she's on her way to the door."

So, I scooted out and scooted around, and I had to go around the stage. I went around the turn, ran flat into somebody and they fell down and I stopped, and I looked around and it was Greta...I was so shocked, I didn't even help her and she—halfway up—she said, "Where were you going?" I was so stunned to be right there having my arms around her, I couldn't say a word. I said, "I'm very sorry." And she said something and got in the car. About fifteen years later, I met her at a party and I told her about it, she remembered it, and she didn't know who I was but she remembered the fall. I still felt the same way. There was something about her. I think in those days, there was something that was a mystery about the word glamour. I don't think anybody knew what the word glamour meant but it was here, and she was a very good example of glamour in a wonderful way. I think in those days there was certain—and here you get back to the word glamour—there was a certain excitement about that. I would sort of get a heavy crush on every girl that was in every picture I did. I mean, it's just that type of thing. It is very exciting. It was quite a time.

Reba: How did you get into the war?

Jimmy Stewart: There was a simple answer to that question, I was drafted. I keep saying it's the only lottery I've ever won in my life. They picked me out just by chance out of three million. I was number 320 so I was right in the first draft.

Reba: Were you ever afraid?

Jimmy Stewart: Yes. Fear was something you had to face all the time. I prayed, not so much for my life but the type of thing they were doing. I was afraid of making a mistake. You could make a mistake in bad weather formation flying. You could make a mistake that would not only cost you your life but maybe four or five airplanes that could get in trouble. Yes, fear was very much a part of this.

Reba: What is your favorite film?

Jimmy Stewart: *It's a Wonderful Life*. Frank Capra and I got together once in a while and talked about it because it was sort of the idea for both of us of picking up where we left off before the war.

But when we got back, Frank picked this picture, it was an idea that somebody just wrote him in a letter, and it was saying things like "no one is born to be a failure" and "no one is poor if he has friends." And it was about those two things and a couple more just little bits. He gave those bits to Hackett and Goodridge, they're one of the best writing teams, and they loved it and they went after it right away and they produced this thing. Frank didn't realize that they could do it that fast and suddenly he found himself with the script and I found myself in the picture. And Frank had a feeling of confidence more than I did as I just wasn't sure whether I knew how to act. I wasn't sure what was going to happen.

Reba: Were you disappointed that it wasn't successful at the time of the release?

Jimmy Stewart: It was quite a disappointment to everybody and especially to Frank. It was very serious to Frank because he had formed Liberty Film, a new company, and the failure of this picture meant the failure of the company, and they all went their own way and it was tragic and it bothered me because it was unsuccessful. But by that time, I'd been in the picture business long enough to know that there is a certain percentage that will fail. And it just wasn't the kind of film that people wanted to see right after the war.

Reba: Surprised with what happened to *It's a Wonderful Life*?

Jimmy Stewart: It somehow didn't surprise me when it started in England even before here. They started picking it up and running it around Christmas ten or twelve years ago and then it started being picked up here. I really think that the feeling here now with young people and old people is entirely different than it was right after the Second World War. I think we've gone through some bad times. We've certainly gone through some good times. I think that the fact that this picture has the value that they see means something to them now. The picture is doing quite well now. It's on cable mostly, and I've heard from the cable people that this is going to continue.

Reba: Where was your career going?

Jimmy Stewart: I think the fact that there was a change in the kind of pictures while I had been away for five years and during that time I had matured and you didn't see it happen slowly, it's sort of came all of a sudden. But once I got started in that direction, then things start going well. I'll always be grateful to Henry Hathaway, who cast me in a picture *Call Northside 777*. I forgot exactly the date it was, but it was a good picture, well written, and Henry one of the best directors. The fact that it was a successful picture gave me some new energy and a new sort of feeling of security. It was almost contemporary when we made it twenty years ago.

The film *The Spirit of St. Louis,* I think the flight itself and Lindbergh really got aviation started in the world as a means of travel. I think before Lindbergh, people never thought travel; they thought of aviators as crazy people like stunt people. They never thought of it as a means to travel, but Lindbergh convinced and showed the world that it could be a means to travel. My agent was producing the picture and he didn't want me because I was too old, which I was. Lindbergh was twenty-seven; I was forty-three. They had another young kid in mind who turned the part down for political reason, Lindbergh favored Germany in the war, and he didn't like that. So, this kid turned down the part and that's when I got the part.

Reba: What came first, *Harvey* or *Winchester 73*?

Jimmy Stewart: I had done *Harvey* and replaced Frank Fey in New York. Frank had been playing it for about four and a half years and he wanted a vacation. I was seeing the play for the first time and the producer, Brock Pemberton, came down between the aisle and said, "How do you like the play?" I said, "It's the most wonderful thing I've ever seen." He said, "Well, why don't you come back and play it for a while?" And I said, "Any time." I thought it was ridiculous that he wanted to talk here between acts, that's fine. I said, "Any time." In two weeks, I was back rehearsing, only I just rehearsed with the producer, then I got to rehearse a day with the cast and did it. I did it two summers because Frank got his vacation one summer and he said, "This is really nice." The next summer I got terrible reviews, it was awful. And Frank said, "Welcome back, I'll bring all the critics back because you've gotten into the part all right." So, I said, "Fine." And they brought all the critics back and I did again. It was worse this time than the last time, but I got sort of the inside track when they sold the picture to the movies. I got the part. And the agent had sort of tagged on this Western as a part of the deal. So, I did *Harvey* and then I went down and just started the Western. So, it was really like winning a horse race, it was really by chance.

Reba: What impact did the Westerns have?

Jimmy Stewart: Well, I think one of the things that's happened, and I don't know whether I strive for this or whether it's just sort of the roles that I fell into. This would happen in Westerns a lot, it's just depended on the story and the plot and my performance and how I felt. When Duke Wayne was in a Western you knew he was going to win. But when I was in something, you just weren't sure. What I hoped would happen is the audience would start pulling for you and say, "Come on now, get going," but they weren't sure. This has been a very good thing for me to hang on to. I'm very glad that *Winchester 73* happened. That happened almost by accident, although people say it was Western comedy; it had a little different flavor then. But I'm glad I got that Western that sort of got me started again. Strange, this was a film that had been around town for years and nobody would touch it and it waited for me.

Reba: At the same time, you're still not married. You took a long time to get married. What did Gloria have...

Jimmy Stewart: Well, I don't know. There was something different, there was something exciting and refreshing when I met her. It's hard to explain. Well, maybe it was sort of the thing that I wanted to do was not marry an actress but to marry someone not in the same profession, I don't know. I don't remember ever considering that, but I just know that once I met her...she always says...I met her, and we started playing golf. We both belong to the same club and so we'd played golf, and after a couple of weeks of having played golf three or four times a week, Gloria turned to me and said, "You know, I eat too. Do you ever think about asking me to dinner? I eat like with knife and fork and everything else." So that got us started and gosh, two or three weeks, I was hooked. We're having so much fun and we're enjoying life too much together to have a divorce.

Reba: What films jump out?

Jimmy Stewart: Well, *Anatomy of A Murder, Flight of The Phoenix*, the Robert Aldrich picture, that was good. I like *The Man from Laramie* Western. And then of course the other Capra picture *Mr. Smith*. I like the Hitchcock pictures. *Rear Window* was such an amazing thing to do to the way he shot the picture and the way he visualized it. Hitchcock created quite a few problems, because some of the shots like shooting to the apartment across the court, he wanted me in focus here and the people over there but in order to do that your depth of field goes all crazy and you have to really clamp down on the lens, which makes it necessary for a whole lot more light. Well, they used all the lights Paramount had and notice that it's not enough, so they borrowed from MGM and Columbia up the street and they got more lights and once it was fine the lights set off the sprinkler system on stage. And Hitchcock got over and sat down in his chair and said, "Well, let's see if you can do something about this and get the rain stopped and, in the meantime, somebody bring me an umbrella."

Reba: Working with Grace Kelly in *Rear Window*?

Jimmy Stewart: Wonderful. You know, this was her fifth picture. She'd never been in the movies before, this was her fifth picture and she was just an enormous star and behaved—everything just worked, and she made it work.

Reba: *Mr. Smith's Goes to Washington* speech?

Jimmy Stewart: We'd been on the speech. I'd been talking for two weeks and Frank said, "Now, you've been talking so long, your voice has to go, and this is a part what I want to do with the scene is to get you so that you finally become unable to talk. Well, I've been going like this sounding hoarse for a day coughing, and at the end of the day Frank came up to me and said, "You don't convince me that you have a sore throat at all, you sound as though you're doing just what you're doing. You're doing this sounding hoarse, you're whispering. It doesn't sound like you have a sore throat," and he walked away. And this really worried me, and I stopped at the doctors on the way home, and I said, "Could you give me a sore throat?" "I really heard that you Hollywood people all have gone off the deep end, but you take the cake. It's taken me twenty-five years to learn how to help people not to have a sore throat. You come in here and want me to give you one? I'll give you the sorest throat anybody ever heard of it," and he said, "Now lay back and open up your mouth." And before I knew it, I had bichloride with mercury in my throat. Well, it turned out that he was fascinated by this and he said, "This won't last very long, but don't worry, I'll be down on the set all day." I don't know what happened to his patients or practice around that time, but he was there all day and it worked. Before he did this, he said, "I'm not getting near your larynx and I'm not going to do any harm, but this is going to irritate your throat."

Reba: And I was wondering how you felt years later to go back to your hometown.

Jimmy Stewart: And that town Indiana, Pennsylvania, had been so close to me all my life; the fact that I haven't been back for several years, the fact that I was seventy-five and I was born and raised there and left when I was quite young. I didn't feel like I had been away. It was wonderful. It was absolutely wonderful. The town wanted the hardware store property and so I decided to put a little sundial right where it used to be, and it's right across from the city hall court house, which is where my statue is, where all the festivities take place. But it was wonderful.

Reba: Do you believe in luck?

Jimmy Stewart: I think luck is connected with superstition. And for me, I'm very superstitious. I'd go twenty-five blocks so I wouldn't have to cross over where a black cat had gone in front of me. And the idea that a hat on the bed, this no good. I just say it's one of these things that I don't think can be ignored. I think you can look back on a lot of things and sort of analyze what happened before, what happened during, and what happened after and who had a part in it, and you can end up and if you're honest with yourself you can look at yourself in the mirror and say, "Brother, you were lucky," period.

Reba: Look back over the body of your work. Would you concede that you are a movie star?

Jimmy Stewart: I like the name movie star all right, but I never thought of myself except to call myself an actor.

Reba: Look back, do you have any regrets?

Jimmy Stewart: Oh, sure, I don't know where to start. Sort of occupation-wise, I'm sorry that I didn't do more theater, sorry that I didn't get back and do more plays. I always thought Hank Fonda had the right idea because it's such a wonderful learning process. It's good discipline, and it's brings you sort up to par when you're maybe sagging and maybe getting a little tired and old, it really brings you right up to your feet.

Reba: Who imitates the best?

Jimmy Stewart: I like Rich Little, and I don't know whether you've ever seen it. I've done it a couple of times. I've enjoyed very much imitating Rich Little imitating me, and I've done pretty good. I've got some laughs out of it—not as many as he had.

My job for *The Glenn Miller Story* was to sell the movie not only in the US but internationally as well. I tried to get as many different stories about what went on behind the scenes when making this film.

Since the film was originally released in 1954 there was no behind the scene footage, so I had to get Mr. Stewart to tell stories that would play well with photo stills from the movie that I had been given. This interview was done before the 57th Academy Awards in March 1985, when he was given an honorary Oscar for fifty years of memorable performances and high ideals on and off the screen. He thanked his directors, fellow performers, his film crews, and the audience who gave him his career. The audience gave him a ten-minute standing ovation.

8
JAMES EARL JONES

Right after Jimmy Stewart, I was sent to interview Chevy Chase for the film *Fletch*. I remember it was a difficult interview for me because he was more interested in getting me and the crew to laugh than answering my questions. It was very frustrating because every time I got a pretty decent answer to my question somehow someone laughed—and a lot of times it was me. If I laughed it would kill the audio track and disrupt the freshness of the original words. Every time I would have to redo a question the response would get flatter and flatter. I was reduced to feeling less than useless, especially if the studio found out. I felt like I was there for hours, and to be honest it stopped being fun. This was so early in my career and very different than doing a talk show, and I feared I had made a mistake. This was the first time in my career that my interviews were being monitored and it was unnerving. I had no control and did not know how to get it back as I didn't want to look incompetent, and most of all, I didn't want to lose the gig. This was a high-stakes game for me, and it would have taken very little to lose my new career. I would have been finished at Universal if Chevy Chase had complained.

After I completed shooting the publicity materials for *The Boys Next Door*, I was offered *Transylvania 6-5000* in Zagreb, Yugoslavia. The film starred Ed Begley Jr., Geena Davis, and Jeff Goldblum, where the latter two met, started their romance, and later would marry. The film *Transylvania 6-5000* was based on the song "Pennsylvania 6-5000" made famous by the Glenn Miller band. The film's script featured Begley and Goldblum as supermarket tabloid writers in search of a Frankenstein monster that was seen in a remote European village.

I brought my own TV crew, and we shot everything we could, not knowing what I would need for the profiles. My video crew, which also included my husband, shot castles, palaces, bustling marketplaces, beautiful flower gardens in the countryside, cobblestone streets and horse-drawn carriages, and captured lots of strangers everywhere we shot. By now all the movies had behind-the-scenes footage, which you will often see as part of the extras on DVDs and in most television- movie publicity. To be on location was exhilarating, exciting, and exhausting as most days were fourteen-to-eighteen hours long. I had to roll with the punches because whatever happened I had to go along with it as I was not allowed to slow down production of the film to get the footage I needed. I'm not really a drama queen, though my family probably thinks I am, so I did what I was told and still managed to be creative.

I started to shoot on the film set of *Soul Man* right after I returned from Yugoslavia. The film starred C. Thomas Howell, Rae Dawn Chong, and James Earl Jones, with the added bonus of the first lady Nancy Reagan and her son Ron, who had a small role. The Reagans screened the film at Camp David and commented through their press secretary that they enjoyed seeing their son in the film.

Reba: Could you describe your character?

James Earl Jones: My character is a Harvard law professor. I think I have to make my character a little bit more off the wall. But he is mature. He has been at it for a long time, teaching law. He loves teaching law. I suspect he probably loves teaching law more than he would love practicing law.

Reba: I really feel that you could be talking about yourself loving to act.

James Earl Jones: Well, I can't say that I like the law. I do love acting. But my first experience with law was in the Army in the days when court-martials were handled, not necessarily by legally trained people. I mean in today's Army every court-martial; the defense and the prosecution are usually lawyers. In my day, this is the Korean War period, junior officers took defense, senior officers took prosecution. It was a mess. Frankly, I get a bad taste in my mouth about law from that.

Reba: What made you decide to try acting?

James Earl Jones: Well, there again, I was on a mountain out in Colorado in the army. I was enjoying it, and my resident commander said, "Well, do you want to go for a captaincy?" I said, "Well, I don't know. My dad is an actor." And he said, "Well, tell you what, why don't you go out and try it? You can always come back to the Army." And went out and tried it and loved it.

Reba: Did it help having a father as an actor, kind of intrigue you?

James Earl Jones: No, my first visit to New York, my dad took me to see a play, Author Miller's *Crucible*. He took me to see a ballet. He took me to see an opera, and he took me to see a comedy, and I loved what was going on up there on the stage. But aside from that, my dad simply made me make my own decisions. He didn't say, "You want to try to be a ballet dancer? You want to try to be an officer?" He just said, "Come see these things with me." But he had no influence on me becoming an actor any more than he did my brother Matthew becoming a musician. He just exposed us to certain things and let us make up our own minds.

Reba: This is a sensitive question, it's about the stuttering. You don't mind talking about it?

James Earl Jones: I don't mind talking about my stuttering because it's just another example of how you find yourself with a weak muscle and you exercise it and sometimes that becomes your strong muscle. It's as simple as that. There are dancers and there are athletes who were once practically crippled and they worked hard to overcome that, and the same way with talking. I was mute from the age of, I forgot the age now, but from the grade one through freshman year in high school. And if you were mute that long, mute because I just gave up on talking, I just say, "I can't cut it." If you're mute that long you become very curious about expressing yourself, you become very in need of a way to express yourself, and for a while I wrote poetry. I found an English teacher in high school who had some insights about what stuttering was and how to work around, and that's what he did. A part of Professor Donald Crouch's insight was that stuttering is a public thing, and if you could find a way that I could express myself privately. He asked me to read my own poetry in front of the English class. I did and I didn't stutter. He said, "Well, there is something to explore there, isn't it?" I was dealing with my own thoughts and my own feelings and I wasn't trying to confront anyone or anything. Later on, I got into the debate class. I was really trying to be upfront, but he started me off in a very private way; speak to yourself. Then I learned to speak to the dog on the farm, the horse on the farm, then I learned to speak to people. But there was always a need to speak or to express within any child, any person, I just had to find mine.

Reba: You were born in the South, do you remember?

James Earl Jones: I was born in Mississippi. Children have very strong memories, and of course, I remember all the things that a child would remember. It was not so much a social problem of Mississippi in the 1930s, those I got through. Those weird bedtime stories that my grandparents would tell us to shock into being good or what they thought was very traumatic life for a black person in the south. As a child, I remember Huck Finn things. I remember catching catfish after a flood in the puddles along the Mississippi River. I remember gathering what we call cheap shock, which was like shamrock, in the woods and would sprinkle salt on it and then eat it, cooking grasshopper legs and eating them. I didn't know the locust cuisine of Africa, but grasshopper had pretty nice taste.

Reba: When you moved to Dublin, Michigan, was it a culture shock for a young boy?

James Earl Jones: The thing I remember was we never rolled Rs in the south. We never pronounced the sound R. When I got to Michigan, even the few black kids that were around, the Indian kids, the Polish kids, they were all going, "Therrre. Herrre." I thought that was funny. It wasn't a shock; it was a joke. I thought, they're killing me.

Reba: What was Michigan like?

James Earl Jones: I guess people associate most life in America with urban life. You think of a black person living in Michigan, they're saying, "So how is Detroit?" "I'm from Mississippi." "Well, how is Jackson?" But farmers lived very independent lives, and we did in Mississippi. We had a farm. Our neighbors were another poor family. They were white people. We didn't associate with them very much, but we were not ghettoized as we think of it in urban life. In Michigan, the same way, we had a farm there, and most of our neighbors were either Indians or Polish kids and Finnish people. And again, we were not ghettoized; we were farmers.

Reba: This role that you're playing has no color, am I right?

James Earl Jones: No, it's important that Professor Rutherford Banks is a black professor because the thrust of the story is a young non- black man experimenting with being black through changes in his pigmentation of his skin and his behavior, hair tone, and so on. So, it's important that Banks is black.

Reba: What advice would you give a young black actor today?

James Earl Jones: I have no advice to give anybody. I think advice is a bad policy. Accepting advice is also bad policy. You can listen to wisdom and you can share wisdom, but I wouldn't give advice to anybody, a young person, except they listen to what they feel they want to do. Advice often can limit someone. If I advise somebody, I'm advising them according to what I know, according to my limitations, and that imposes limitations on them. I wouldn't do it.

I wanted to interview James Earl Jones, the voice that everyone knew and recognized. It was an excellent opportunity to share the story of how a child with a terrible stutter would own the world with his voice as Darth Vader from *Star Wars*.

There were protests that took place within the Black community when the movie opened. *Soul Man* was supposed to be a comedy, but to the public it was a racist statement and not the least bit humorous. It's interesting, they wanted to make a comedy and instead they made a controversy. I never forgot the release of this film because of that, but I wonder who got the last laugh as *Soul Man* was a box-office success.

Of course, there was a music video release for *Soul Man* performed by Sam Moore and Lou Reed. Later the song got inducted into the national recording Registry of the Library of Congress. It is because of the cultural, historic, and aesthetic importance to the national recorded sound that mirrored our lives.

9
ARNOLD SCHWARZENEGGER

I was excited with butterflies in my stomach when I got my first major studio film, *'night Mother*, starring Anne Bancroft, shooting all the video publicity materials, including behind-the-scenes as well as interviews. I was getting used to being on film sets, but this time I would be working on two films at the same time and one was a union shoot, which was a different story. This was the first action film I worked on from a major studio. All my other work had been small films, mostly independent ones. I had never been on a major studio film set and hoped it was like the independent ones; I did not want anybody to know that I did not know the rules of protocol. I didn't want to make any mistakes. I was told by the studio that I had to join the publicist guild, a recognized union that would allow me on union film sets, and it cost $1,500 to be paid by me before I could be given the film. My crew had to belong to a union as well. I had to show credentials for the crew and myself. After *'night Mother*, I was prepared to go to any union film set and was ready for Arnold and his film *The Running Man*.

There is an old saying that great things come in small packages, but that doesn't apply to Arnold Schwarzenegger. There was nothing small about this man. I didn't know what to expect when I met him on the *The Running Man* set, but nothing could have prepared me for what I got. My first encounter with him was a handshake, which surprised me as he had very soft hands, and then a lovely gentle hug. I loved it, as I expected him to crush me because he was so strong. Everything about Arnold surprised me, including his willingness to talk.

Reba: I found fascinating your attitude that you can do anything you set your mind to. How much of it came from body building?

Arnold Schwarzenegger: When you're involved in sports as much as I have been you learn a lot of things about yourself. I mean, developing your body is one thing, but there is a tremendous amount of discipline. For instance, you also get a lot of self-confidence from a training and you know, you can do anything. As you gain the self-confidence through sports and if you visualize your goals, they became reality the same with movies.

This is why I feel very strongly about the kids getting into sports because the things you learn, the camaraderie, the discipline, the self- respect, and the confidence—all the things that you learned from sports. It's just something that you can never learn anywhere else; not in the school, not through your parents, you only learn by doing sports.

Reba: When you first started, you were fifteen years old. Were your parents supportive?

Arnold Schwarzenegger: My father and mother supported the whole idea of doing sports a lot, but they always wanted to make sure that there is a balance between sports and education. In my case, I wanted to play soccer so they always would keep a balance and to keep down the sport and emphasize the education.

When I got into bodybuilding and into weightlifting, I didn't have much support at all from my parents because they didn't understand it, nor did anyone else because in Austria weightlifting was known, but not bodybuilding and power lifting. And when I won the first competition, my parents were very proud when I came home with my first trophy. They were very proud and running all over the village with the trophy and saying, this is my son here, look at this. He's already winning championships.

Reba: How do you make yourself look different?

Arnold Schwarzenegger: When you have the power of visualization and then turning that vision that you have into reality, which you get from sports, you can apply it to anything else. You visualize that. All of a sudden you become very well-mannered, and your hair looks different, you trim down your body, which is very easy for me to do, to go down with the body weight. Twenty pounds of it gone, whereas other people would have to go into severe diets or go and get a tummy tuck or vacuum job around their stomach to get them waist slim. I just do it with just a little bit of diet and training and then within a month it works.

Reba: Are you comfortable with comedy?

Arnold Schwarzenegger: Comedy is something that is a very natural thing for me because in real life I always had a great sense of humor and even when we worked out four or five hours a day and everyone was really grim and serious about doing another set of lifting 400 pounds and they had those facial expressions of intensity. To me it was a fun time in the gym, and we were always joking around. I always wanted to bring that kind of sense of humor into the film. And so that's why my humor is always in it. Eventually down the line, I will do a straight comedy. I'm sure of that. I just tried to kind of ease in the audience and bring them along to that side of me.

Reba: You don't fit what Hollywood would consider a leading man?

Arnold Schwarzenegger: In order to make it to the top in anything is to be unique and not to fall into the mode of everyone else. If I would have looked like a million other people in the acting industry, I would not have made it because you're competing then with a million other guys. If you talk about my name being a disadvantage because it's hard to pronounce, I made it into an advantage and people say my body was a disadvantage because I only can play big, strong guys, I made it to my advantage. And when they say, listen to your accent, you know, it's very hard to sell your accent in America, I made it to my advantage because I realized that America is not just Americans, it's a patch quilt, this country, with a lot of foreigners, with Spanish and with the French and with the Japanese and people from all over the world have settled here. And so, I made all those kinds of obstacles into an advantage and it really worked and now those things are really a big asset because people write scripts now for me and tailor it around me. I never felt it was a disadvantage.

Reba: How did you start here?

Arnold Schwarzenegger: I came to this country with nothing and I was just a bodybuilder that has won the World championships, the Mr. Universe contest. America was known as the country of opportunities and I wanted to take advantage of that and be part of it. I mean, I could go on for hours to tell you how great America is because I really come from a whole different side.

Reba: When you became an American citizen, what went through your head?

Arnold Schwarzenegger: It takes years. And so, by the time you get it, you've looked forward to it so much that it's one of the most delightful moments. I will always remember when you're sworn in. I celebrated it much more so than any movie opening I've ever had, any birthday party I've ever had or anything else that I've done because it was a big moment in my life, and I felt that now I'm part of a country that I respect so much and that I think is a real winning team and has the best ormula economically and politically. And so, I was proud, you know, 've felt like running around afterwards and screaming, "I am an merican."

Reba: You don't mind promoting your movies.

Arnold chwarzenegger: The interest that I have in making a movie successful is just simply because I don't want to work on a movie for a year, act in it, rehearse the stunts, take my life through dangerous events with action stuff, and then have it go in the toilet. I mean, who wants that? I don't want it because first of all, it is not fair to do to me.

And second, it isn't fair to the studio that puts the million dollars into the movie so everyone should make their money back and add on and make much more out of it. And I was lucky the last four or five movies of mine made a lot of money. So, the studios are very happy to come back to me and say let's do another one. Now that's a great compliment.

Reba: You're always very optimistic, very cheerful.

Arnold Schwarzenegger: I tell you, when you look at my life, I must be a big idiot if I will be depressed because I have a wonderful wife, the best woman that I ever could have. I have a great job. I do exactly what I want, which is acting. I've had a great bodybuilding career. I was traveling all over the world. I have plenty of money, and I have a lot of fun and I do my little extra activities of charitable events where I can help people and stuff. I have everything so everything is going so well for me and I live in the best country in the world, how can I be a down or negative or anything like that? Of course, everyone has its ups and downs in the career but overall, I feel it's just wonderful the way everything is going.

Reba: You have a highly publicized marriage. When you went into the marriage you knew that she was going to pursue a career.

Arnold Schwarzenegger: I moved to America and I changed very quickly. First of all, because it was necessary to change and have an open mind and realize that women also want to have a career and go out and do the kind of things that I like to do. I started to appreciate women who had much more to say than to talk about just the kids and about the home and stuff like that. And I got addicted actually to that. I mean, it's wonderful when you marry the woman who has an interesting job. So also it's very exciting when it's a smart woman, a woman that has a great personality, that has also goals that she is pursuing. So, to me, it became a great asset and I couldn't imagine doing it any other way.

Reba: Are you tolerant of people that do not have your drive?

Arnold Schwarzenegger: Yes, because not everyone can have a drive. So, there are many different kinds of people around. You cannot expect everyone to be the same. And it is also an advantage if everyone is not the same because it makes it easier for me. Can you imagine if everyone would be like me, out there trying to conquer the world and climbing up that ladder and all those things? So, it's perfect the way it is. Believe me. And the only thing is that when you have people working around you, you want to get the job done and you want efficiency because you hire them for this kind of purpose and then you get maybe a little bit intolerant if they do not work as fast or think as fast. I appear very calm and not intense but I actually, when it comes to work, I am very intense, and I expect a lot from people that are around me.

Reba: Is success everything you thought it was going to be?

Arnold Schwarzenegger: I've never really thought of it as now I have to be successful, now I have to be a star. There's all kind of things that come with it. What is more important to me is that if I visualize the goal and if I have something in mind that I want to achieve, I'll go after it. I didn't really care, but what is important to me is that I do the things that I want to do and if I set a goal and I go after it, and then if that happens to be successful by everyone's point of view, great, it's an added-on thing, but that's really not the major purpose.

Reba: Is there any chance we in California might have a political part of you?

Arnold Schwarzenegger: I'm very much interested in politics. I'm very much interested in economics, but I have no interest in running for office, if that's what you're asking me. No, I have no interest. There's so much more to do in the entertainment business and then producing and directing and then acting and so on that there's no room in it. But still I'm interested in the subject.

Besides doing the interview, I was responsible for getting everyone, including the film crew, to sign releases, which included

Arnold. However, Arnold's publicist, Charlotte Parker, redacted everything on the release form about uses for his interview, though Arnold didn't care. Before I started this book, I ran into Charlotte Parker at a women's conference and told her about the book and how much I wanted to use that interview over all the other ones I had done with him, and she said, "Use it with my blessing."

After that first film, I interviewed him for *Jungle All the Way*, *End of Days*, *Collateral Damage*, and *Terminator 3: The Rise Of the Machines*, and he actually remembered me. I also did an interview with him when he became the chairman on the President's Council for Physical Fitness and Sports in 1993, and I brought up *The Running Man* electronic press kit. He said that he enjoyed the interview. That's what I liked about Arnold Schwarzenegger; he made you feel important for that moment even if he didn't remember you.

The year 1987 started out with a bang, first with Arnold's
The Running Man and then shooting the publicity materials
on the Meryl Streep film *Iron Weed*, costarring Jack Nicholson. The film was being shot in upstate New York, and I was
given a lot of time to get the footage I needed. The contract pro-
hibited me from interviewing Jack Nicholson, so what I did—and
he doesn't know it—was shoot footage of him working on the
set. Nicholson really liked us and as long as my cameraman
had his camera facing the ground, he would hang out with us.
He told us stories about Hollywood, making us laugh and
giving us a good time. The behind-the-scenes footage, now part
of the Reba Merrill Collection, can be found at the Motion Picture Academy Archive.

My crew and I were told that we would interview Meryl Streep
before she started shooting at 11:00 a.m. We came to the set early and
awaited her arrival. I was unprepared when she walked in to do the
interview with wet hair, no makeup, and glasses. I told her this video
interview was going to last long after the film was released in case she
wanted to put on some makeup—she thought the interview was for
print. She ended up turning down the interview. When I got back to
Los Angeles, I had interviewed neither star of the film and I wondered
what was going to happen to me and my job. It took a long time for
Meryl Streep to let me interview her again, which I did in New York at
a Madison Avenue hotel. She insisted that the studio hire Roy Holland,
who was paid $1,500, to do her hair and makeup. In fact, he does all of
her hair and makeup, and won an Oscar for his work on the film *Iron
Lady*. Meryl did not put any restrictions on time or the questions. I just

kept asking questions and before I knew it, we had talked for an hour.

Reba: Are you the first one in show business?

Meryl Streep: I'm the first one in show business in my family, but I've dragged many along with me now. I mean, my little brother is a dancer and a choreographer , let's see, who else is in the business? My son wants to be an actor now.

Reba: Did your family react, I guess positively, or as the firstborn, were you allowed to just do anything?

Meryl Streep: Was I allowed to do anything I wanted as the first-born? Is the firstborn allowed to do anything? No, the lastborn is allowed to do anything. The firstborn is the one they try to inflict on you rules and then everything deteriorates and the last one gets to do whatever they want. No, my parents were very supportive. I don't know why; I really just think it's their breadth of imagination. They just didn't think that was a bad idea at all.

Reba: When did you decide to be an actress?

Meryl Streep: I decided to be an actress halfway through drama school. I'd already invested a lot of time and money in it, and it was something that was hard to commit to because I didn't think it was a serious sort of way to spend your life and one that would help the world and everything else that we all wanted to do then. But now I think my mind has changed about that, and I think it is a valuable thing.

Reba: We need actors with passion and commitment to speak out.

Meryl Streep: Well, I think that's important. I suppose that's become a very important part of being a famous person or a celebrity is that you can speak out on things that bother them, especially people who are more knowledgeable than maybe I am on a certain thing.

Reba: Most of the time when you commit to a movie, you stay in character. Did it make it difficult to work and leave weeks at a time?

Meryl Streep: In this film, I had a lot of time off. I mean, I sort of was looking for a project that I could do with three children and one very new baby. My daughter, Grace, had just been born five months before I started preparing for this part, so I thought this was perfect. They were shooting an hour and a half from where I lived. I had three days of work, and a week off, and it ended up being the most difficult kind of schizophrenic endeavor imaginable because it was. Just that immersion in the actual work does your work for you? I mean, when they pick you up at six in the morning every morning and dumped you back home at eight at night every single day. It was very disconcerting, and I had to exercise a lot more concentration and actual work than I usually count on doing in the middle of a project. In Africa, I was there for 120 days and I was never off except on the day off. And on that day, I could just sort of lie down with a towel on my head, you know, and breathe deeply and then we would start again, but actually made it easier to stay connected to the project. This was tougher because I got real involved in projects at home, you know every single piece of clothing I had is ruined by arts and crafts, things. And I was home a lot with my kids playing and doing all the other things that I'm supposed to be doing as a mother, and I didn't just cut it off the way I usually did so it was very hard to go in.

Reba: Is it easier when you go into a film with somebody you've worked with before or does it not matter?

Meryl Streep: In some ways it's easier, but in some ways, it makes you assume things that you probably shouldn't assume. Working with Jack again—he's very unpredictable and yet I trust him like forever. And I think that that's the basis of the best work is when you know anything you throw out there is going to be picked up and returned and you can accept it for whatever it is? I hate to be so general. What I like about working with him is his sense of humor in such an intense piece as this is, which is very different from *Heartburn*. He just has a lot of energy. He just throws off sparks so it's exciting to work with him and it's fun to work with him. So, I enjoy it on that level. But as far as knowing what he's going to do next because of the fact that we've worked together and we're friends, I don't know that. He's surprising on screen.

Reba: All your characters have strength.

Meryl Streep: You're right. The women that they make movies about are the strong women, for one, and those are the jobs that are out there. I've been accused of playing always victims, but I've always said, "That's also who they make the movies about." They make movies about women who were killed, murdered, otherwise psychologically maimed. Who knows why? I mean, it's drama. That's conflict. And that's what's around. And basically, I've never produced. I take the jobs that are out there and so that's what's there.

Reba: Has it crossed your mind to produce?

Meryl Streep: I have trouble telling the babysitter what I really wanted her to do. I can't tell somebody, "Do you mind going in that closet and getting those dust balls? I would do it, but I just don't have time. I'm going to go out now." I can't delegate. I have to do it all myself. I would be the most horrible producer. Who has that many hours in the day? I have three children, little children, and they don't want a memo from me. They want me, and I don't know how the people do it that have kids and produce. I hate the telephone. I would rather, you know, commit a crime than talk on the telephone basically. And that's what producers do. It's completely boring to me, the prospect of that. And I really am glad that I've worked with such wonderful producers and I have, and I've been extremely lucky with the directors and producers that I've worked with because they've taken care of all that and I come in and I do my work, which I love to do, but when I go home I don't have to worry if they have the money for the teamsters or if the food has salmonella or if so and so's deal fell through and they're in Aruba and we need somebody to play the second lead. I couldn't care less about that.

Reba: You play a classical piece in the piano store scene. Was it difficult to learn?

Meryl Streep: I had to learn this piece and Hector said, "It's a very simple piece, you know, very simple, Scriabin." And it's beautiful for my character who's sort of like this bird, but it's incredibly difficult, anyway. My kids would come in every day and they bang on the ends of the piano and I'm there trying to get the thing and I found it really impossible to learn it and I kept telling Hector that it was impossible. He said, "It's a very simple piece, no big deal," and we got to the day and he actually believed that I am super woman and that I could play it and I came in, I said, "I actually can't play this. I can't play." He said, "You can't? I said, "No, I can't. I can pretend to play it and you'll have to mute the piano and I can actually mime with Horowitz. But if you hear what it is that I'm actually playing, people will run screaming from the theater." So, he muted the piano and we did the scene and my hands matching what's happening on the record. But if you actually heard it, it's hideous.

Reba: Acting, it's a profession, but it is a craft.

Meryl Streep: Yes, it is a craft. A lot of people don't want to talk about that part. Especially somebody like me who's accused of being crafty, you know, technical. And that's because of these accents that I've been obliged to use. But I don't throw them in, I don't think arbitrarily. I use them; if the film comes from Denmark, I try not to sound like I come from Somerville, New Jersey. But I think craft is important. It has been to me, just as another a color on your palate. Anything that affords you a wider range of choices I think is good. Physical stamina is good, an interesting voice is good. Cultivating a certain interesting voice like some people do is good because all the things that help you build up your little toolbox are all the things that make it easier for you to create illusion, and that's what it's about, really. It's easier to talk about the tools than to talk about the illusion. And I think education for an actor depends on what kind of actor you want to be. If you want to move around on all sorts of different stages, sound stages and theatrical stages, it's important for you to have this instrument that's variable. If you're not interested in that, you don't have to go to drama school and all that jazz. If you have a wonderful personality that people like, then you can be—just present that and it's irresistible.

Reba: Is acting important?

Meryl Streep: I have a theory that this is why we permit actors to exist in our midst, is that everybody in their childhood has that. It's very interesting to me—what is it in human beings that would share emotions? What is empathy? What is the thing that makes you sit in a darkened theater and watched somebody go through something very tough and hard and makes you cry? The fact that we are that connected to one another as human beings is a good starting point in a world where sometimes it seems like we're all so isolated from each other. And art is a kind of, at least cinema, a unifying experience. It can be. I think it is at this point for me. I'm glad that I took it up and I'm not so pragmatic in thinking that it's useless and just narcissistic because it doesn't enrich people's lives.

Reba: I want to know why you have the fear that you won't get offered anything.

Meryl Streep: You do have the fear, plus you have the fear you won't get offered anything even after that job. You have that fear of the second job, a third job, fourth job. You have it all the way down the line. I saw an interview with Alec Guinness, who thought he'd never work again after *Star Wars* or something, right? Because the fear is always there with actors that you'll never work again. That goes with the territory.

Reba: Do you feel that too? You are Meryl Streep. Do you feel that you may never work again?

Meryl Streep: No. I saved up my money now if I don't work again. Yes, of course, I feel that. I feel that every time I read Pauline Kael. Sure, but now I think, well, if I save up enough money, I don't have to worry.

Reba: Does it bother you? Do reviews bother you? Do you care?

Meryl Streep: Oh, yes, I care. Are you kidding? Of course, I care.

Reba: The bad reviews or get the good one?

Meryl Streep: You forget the good ones. You only remember the bad ones.

Reba: What would you have done if you didn't act?

Meryl Streep: I probably would have tried to do something in design. I took my degree from Vassar in costume design. Or some sort of commercial art or an illustrator or something like that.

Reba: When you first started out, you did struggle?

Meryl Streep: No, I had a lot of lucky breaks early on. I didn't know that, and the future seemed unknown to me, even though now with the benefit of hindsight, I can look back and say that led to that, led to that, led to that, but it didn't necessarily have to. Lots of people opening in a show at the public theater like I did, and nothing happens, it's just a series of a fortuitous coincidences and breaks and that's how fate works.

Reba: So, when you're working on a project, do you feel things as an actress?

Meryl Streep: I remember sitting down on the couch in the loft downtown, I said to my husband in the middle of *Sophie's Choice*, I said, "I have a feeling about this. It's just, I'm so proud of it." This is ight in the middle and I'm really very superstitious, so I don't like to o that sort of thing, but I just said, "I'm so filled up with this one and I'm so happy. I mean if it isn't totally wonderful, it's just going to be the most horrible plummeting disappointment." And that one ended up being very satisfying artistically, even the year and a half you have to wait until it comes out. But from the time I made it to the time I saw it, there was no sort of letdown. Sometimes there is. Sometimes there's a funny kind of distancing that you thought it was one thing and it becomes something completely different. In terms of *Out of Africa*, I always knew that that was something that I'd like to see because I just wanted to see that place again. I mean, the place was almost as big a character as any of the people in it. And over the time that we had to wait to see that I was surprised by how much the story, how much weight it had. I thought it was going to be more like a travel log experience with aristocratic people in it. But it was more heart than I ever imagined came through. And that was very gratifying. But you can't tell in the beginning.

Reba: How you deal with loss of privacy?

Meryl Streep: How do I deal with losing privacy? I don't know. I don't know a good answer to that. I think it's really hard knowing this is going to be broadcast millions of years from today. But I don't have that problem, and needless to say, I don't like a loss of privacy. My privacy is important to me. It's even more important to my husband. Because by the nature of the work he does, he's likes to work solitary without distractions. So ,we moved out of the city, for one thing. That helps.

Reba: Do you have a lot of disciplines? You look very disciplined to me.

Meryl Streep: Why do I look disciplined to you?

Reba: You showed up here and on a movie set.

Meryl Streep: I show up at a movie set; I get paid. I mean, this interview is part of the job. The production company will tell you this is the only thing I'm doing. I'm not so good at promoting my films.

Reba: A good memory?

Meryl Streep: It's a good memory. It's a very quick flash memory. It's not a retentive memory. I have a very quick ear and I imagine and recreate those situations quickly. I have an ear that I can pick up how people sound. And as I said, it's sort of one of my tools. It's like a musical sense; it's very aligned with that. People who are good with languages have that same ability.

Reba: But you could have been a singer if you wanted to.

Meryl Streep: I could have been the contender. Yeah, I would like to have been a singer. In fact, I'd love to have been Frederica von Stade.

Reba: What would you consider your big break?

Meryl Streep: Well, probably Rosemary Tisher at the Public Theater giving me an audition after the deadline was passed. They do these public auditions; anybody can come in. At that time, they did at the Public Theater in New York City. Everybody in my drama class prepared for these auditions and they all went down to New York and did them, I had a nervous stomach, and I couldn't go. But basically, I knew that I just didn't want to be in that whole meat market, and also that competition makes me very nervous, so I just called her up and said—asked her and pleaded with her to see me some other time. And she did, and I don't know why, she just is a nice woman and she gave me an audition and based on that I got another audition with Joe Papp and he hired me for *Trelawny of the "Wells,"* which was being done at Lincoln Center that fall. That was right after drama school. That was a big break.

Reba: Did you get nervous auditioning in your early days?

Meryl Streep: I still get nervous, very nervous if I have to audition. If I have to sing in front of people, if I have to go on an awards thing. If I have to speak, impromptu speak, I'm just terrified. I'm much more comfortable enclosed in a world of fiction.

Reba: Do you have any regrets?

Meryl Streep: Yes, I regret that I didn't move out of town sooner. I think I wasted a lot of time being nervous and uptight walking around in this sort of highly charged—it's not sort of my kind of energy.

Reba: Do you believe in luck?

Meryl Streep: Of course, yes, if there's anything to believe in. I mean, it's not a deity; it's just series of circumstances, yes. I mean, it happens.

Reba: Do you think you make your own? I know you made *Sophie's Choice* happen for you because I read that story that they were going to cast an eastern European woman.

Meryl Streep: I didn't make anything happen. They do what they want basically, these guys, you know, they do. And I really wanted to play Sophie, but I didn't bite anybody's ankle to get the part, I just said, "Give me a chance to read for it."

Reba: Is success everything you thought it was going to be?

Meryl Streep: I never imagined in my wildest dream that I would successful. So each sort of happy event as it happened has been a surprise. I'm Damocles with the sword, you know, I really think it's up there by a hair, and every day it doesn't happen I'm just thrilled, but I don't, you know, I never thought it was going to happen to me. You can't if you're an actor. Some people do I guess, go in and say, "I'm going to be a star," and they are. But for all those people that say that I bet there are hundreds of thousands who say that and are still struggling. And I know a lot of my success has to do with luck. I've also poured a lot of hard work into it so I feel in some way that I can justify myself ? But I'm just happy that things have happened this way. Personally, because the greatest break in my life was when I met Don Gummer, so I mean, there's no question in my mind about that.

After the interview was over, I told Meryl I would send her a transcript and a VCR of the interview that I wanted to use for her to approve of. She was going to be in Australia working on *Cry in the Dark* when this film was going to be released. She followed through and sent me back the transcript with the deleted portions.

I was taken aback when I received a call from the former studio executive who had propositioned me years before. He had been brought in as a consultant on *Ironweed* and demanded all the footage. I told him he could only have what she had approved. I felt it was the honorable thing to do—keep my word to her. He threatened me numerous times over this to the point that I called my lawyer Harold Lipton to take care of the situation.

To this day I have no idea what my lawyer told the production company, but I was able to finish the job I was hired to do. Mr. Self-Important still had to get the last word in. He called to tell me how much harm I had caused myself by not turning over the footage. He promised me he would personally make sure no one else would ever hire me and added, "You will never work in this town again." He was right to an extent, as a lot of his friends' production companies hired and then fired me before I even started. Lucky for me there were many companies and studios where he had no power, so I got to work for another twenty years. It's been thirty-two years since I did the interview with Meryl Streep, and when I went to the screening and party for her film *Little Women,* I told her what happened. Stars like Streep never hear the behind-the-scenes stories, and she told me how surprised she was that I was willing to fight for her interview and possibly risk my career. I am so glad that I was finally able to tell her what happened.

11
MIKE NICHOLS

I was given both of the Neil Simon films, at the same time, that Universal was bringing to the screen. The first film was *Brighton Beach Memoirs,* which took me to New York. I took my approved video crew with me. The studio did not complain; this was before the accountants took over Hollywood. Those travel expenses, including my husband as part of my crew, were covered. Later I learned I could have picked up crews all over the world; I was so new to working on union films it never occurred to me. But there is something to be said for working with people that were familiar with your style.

After shooting for a week in New York, I was off to Bordeaux with my Los Angeles crew to shoot interviews and behind the scenes on *Flagrant Désir* starring Sam Waterston, Lauren Hutton, and Marisa Berenson. This shoot was one I never forgot as wine was served at lunch, which never happens on US film sets, and of course the food was divine. The biggest surprise took place when we were shooting at a winery and the owners invited me and my entire crew to dinner at their château along with the stars of the film. It was fabulous. Then it was back to New York to finish shooting for *Brighton Beach Memoirs.* Although it did not go on to do well at the box office, I had already been given *Biloxi Blues* slated to begin shooting in 1987 with the Oscar winning director Mike Nichols.

Reba: Why this film?

Mike Nichols: I think it had to do with my connection with Neil Simon. I always thought that Neil could write something that was completely a movie but didn't have even a trace of its history as a play. And I thought that Biloxi was that story that came right from Neil, but it's a movie more than a play. It was always a movie more than a play. And the theme of becoming a man is forever interesting. I think it's one of the most interesting themes, but I also think that our themes choose us. I don't really know a lot about the themes of my work.

I recently saw a sort of a retrospective thing. I was talking to a group of film students and I saw clips from my pictures on most of which I hadn't seen since we shot them. And I felt quite outside of it. I felt like, "Oh, I see this guy was interested in this and this and this and this." Things that I didn't know about.

Reba: Is it an instinct that you're feeling when you direct a project?

Mike Nichols: Well, I think it's a number of things, but I think there's the technical aspect of the craft, the practical things that you need to know and that you do as a sort of way of priming the pump for the instinctual things. In other words, there are certain things that you have to do like getting your lunchbox and showing up for work on time and punching your card and all the things we do on the way to work. Those are the things the director does. You have to cast the picture and you have to decide where you shoot it and what it is physically. Most important, you have to decide what's the physical expression of all the aspects of the story. Where is the camera? What's happening in front of the camera? Who's where? What does the camera do? Is it up? Is it down? Does it move? These decisions that are based on what you're telling, what your story is.

If you're good in a few lucky decisions some things happen to you that you didn't expect. I mean, my extreme example as always, it's the end of *The Graduate* and I had a nice time making the picture. I was very gentle with them. We were shooting the last scene in which Dustin and Katharine run from the church and get on the bus. The script simply said they get on the bus and look out the back window and to my own surprise, I found myself saying to them, "Now, listen, we've stopped traffic for twenty blocks and we have cops in front of the bus, now you get on that bus and laugh," and they both started to cry. And I thought, "What is wrong with me? Why am I doing this to them?" And they did the scene and the next day I saw the dailies and they were so terror-stricken with tears in their eyes. And I thought, "Oh, look, this is the end of the picture." I discovered that I behaved badly when we shot it. Then I discovered, I suppose, an unconscious reason for behaving in this uncharacteristic way. And there they were onscreen terrified of the future, dumbstruck, unable to say anything to each other, unable to laugh. And it's the whole thing in any of the work any of us has done is that those are the things you can pray for it, but you can't make them come.

Reba: Actors have a tendency to remain childlike for life.

Mike Nichols: Well, I think they need to. They have to keep coming to everything for the first time.

Reba: Does it give you an edge, once being on the other side of the camera?

Mike Nichols: I think there's no question that for a director to have been an actor or be an actor is one of the most useful things for several reasons. One reason is that you know what it feels like to be an actor. You know what's possible. You know what's not possible for an actor, and you have respect for the sort of mysteries of that process to do it for the first time. But also, if you were a good performer, you have a clock in you. And the clock, I think, is the most important thing for the work we do.

Reba: Do you think you were born funny?

Mike Nichols: I saw two of my kids born. They were born as they were going to be. You know, like my son, who is a little like me, came out complicated and analyzing things and a little worried about how the whole thing had gone and also funny. You know, my daughter came out and thanked everybody and was very grateful to everybody in the sort of delivery room and then asked her where she could have her hair done and that was it. I think we are going to be as we're going to be. I don't think you can get funny. I think it's a gift. As all these things are. God gives you certain gifts.

Reba: *Barefoot in the Park* was first. How in the world did you know you could direct?

Mike Nichols: I didn't know I could direct; it was somebody else's idea. It was Saint Subber, the producer's idea, that I should direct, and I thought, "Well, why not try?" And on the very first day of rehearsal, on the first five minutes of the first day of rehearsal, I thought, "Look at this. This is what I've been getting ready to do all the time, but I didn't know it. This is what I was learning from Strasburg when I didn't know that was what I was learning. This is what I was learning being an improvisational comedian for all those years because I was learning what makes a scene and what is it that happens between people to make a scene." And I felt instantly that I'd come home, something I'd never felt before in work. Even when Elaine and I were big comics and we were very successful and everybody wanted us to be here and be there and be on television, be on Broadway, I always thought of it as sort of a great way to make money until I started the grownup part of my life. And then this turned out to be the grownup part of my life.

Reba: Was there air of excitement or fear, or a combination of both?

Mike Nichols: Excitement, no fear, because it's sort of like the first time you make love to somebody that you're meant for is that you know everything is great. It was absolutely great. I knew when I've walked into that theater two minutes after we started that rehearsal, I knew that I knew what to do.

Reba: Okay. I guess you don't miss performing, or are you performing as a director?

Mike Nichols: It's possible, but I think I have another way of thinking about it. I think that there's a secret about directing that's fairly well kept. Naturally, should I reveal it. To me, acting, as you say, is the childlike portion of all of us. It is, in the best sense, childlike.

It's innocent and it's new and it's coming to stuff for the first time. Directing is the daddy part of all this, and what the secret of directing is that if someone is being daddy, it's as reassuring as though someone was being daddy for you. It doesn't matter who is daddy as long as the process is taking place. It is very reassuring to be the father on the set, to be the one that everybody turns to because you think, yeah, right, I do know what I want. I know what to do and it's going to be okay. It's like driving as opposed to being driven. Would you rather drive than have somebody else drive you?

Reba: What you're really saying is that you like control?

Mike Nichols: Yes, that's right. I love control, and I love losing control or giving up control.

Reba: Aren't you saying two different things?

Mike Nichols: Well, all interesting ideas are two opposite things held in suspension. You can't just say one. Control by itself is monstrous, and lack of control by itself is out of the question. What you pray for is both, is that you have control of the things you need to control, but you can give up control to a situation in which someone else might have to control it or no one or someone you love.

Reba: You are on a roll. Does that put pressure on you?

Mike Nichols: I think of it another way. I think of it as a pendulum. If you're talking about success in show biz, it's a pendulum. Very successful, you swing up. Not so successful, you swing back. We all swing back and forth. And each swing of the pendulum as you're going into another award or whatever it is, it's gathering force for the swing back. I think both are interesting and both are lucky and each leads to the other. In the end you know when you've done enough stuff that people respect and you respect yourself and you don't have to work quite as hard to make a living and so on, you end up wanting to do something you can be proud of, which is really the same thing that you want for your kids, and it's great to see your kids beginning to be proud of things they can do and it's great to be a little proud of things you've done yourself and then to aim for something maybe that you can't do.

Reba: Directing, did you know if you could pull it off?

Mike Nichols: I have a very specific ambition, which I didn't know I had. I never know anything, I think, until people asked me. At this film student thing, somebody said, "what is your ambition?" I said, "I guess my ambition is to make a movie of which people say, 'can you do that? I don't think you can do that.'"

Reba: What do you think you could do?

Mike Nichols: To me, making movies is the highest calling for a man. I can't think of anything I would rather do than that. And I love doing plays. I love my life, and it's very hard to imagine another one. I think that if I couldn't do those two jobs, I would probably just sort of traveled around and look at things and pick up dish-washing jobs and so forth as I'm going. I don't think I would want to work in an office.

Reba: Do you believe luck played a part?

Mike Nichols: Oh, sure. Well, anatomy is faith as we know from Freud, but luck is everything and you can't ever forget that all the things that you think is so terrific about yourself are in fact luck and that you got to still continue to be glad of your luck every day.

Reba: Is success everything you thought it would be?

Mike Nichols: I don't really know what success is. It's nice as everybody's always saying, it's very nice to get a table in the restaurant, and it's very nice to have money to get the stuff that you'd want to be relatively secure and take care of your family and so forth. It's all a delicate balance because as we all know, if you get too much of anything, it's as bad as having too little of anything. So, what I'm left with is the same thing. I started out with what Elaine May and I used to know together; the only safe thing is to take a chance.

Reba: I get the feeling that directing a movie is that you can control everything.

Mike Nichols: You try to control everything. It's like life; a lot of things that you can't control. Part of it is trusting other people. I implicitly trust that the people I work with who knows what they're doing and if you work with, say, Meryl Streep or Jack Nicholson, the whole trick is to make it possible for them to do what they do and not get in the way. I'm not going to show up and say to Meryl, "Now, remember, you hate this guy, and this is how mad I want you to get. And when you say the word so and so, let me see you look really disappointed." That'd be crazy. I'd be destroying one of the great gifts ever anywhere. The whole thing is to try and make a place that's nice for people to come to every day and where they can do what they do.

Reba: When you saw that off-Broadway performance of Whoopi Goldberg—wasn't even off-Broadway, it was somewhere, what did you see?

Mike Nichols: I saw a great artist. I saw an artist, but I also saw that thing that you just can't miss when you see it if that's what you're good at seeing. It's just somebody who can walk right through any crowd right up to anybody she wants to and have what she wants. There are angels, you know, there are people who are angels who just walk through the rest of us able to say what they mean and do what they want: Whoopi is, Meryl is. I have a kid like this, and I've seen it all her life. She just is very simple and truthful with people and gets what she wants because she never wants anything that takes anything away from anyone else. And when you see such a person, it's someone who can bring a lot of pleasure to people because they can tell us the truth, which is still the best thing to hear.

Reba: When you worked with Cher, she was very frightened. How did you put her at ease?

Mike Nichols: Well, the director's main job really is to say, "What's happening here is this. This is what's happening." Now, how do we create that thing that's happening? I mean, it's funny, in seeing these films at this retrospective thing… In fact, there was a scene from Silkwood, not one of Cher's scenes, but a scene in which Meryl had just washed her hair and she was doing her nails and Kurt was on the bed and somehow Meryl didn't get on the bed and she ended up in the kitchen and he finally went to the kitchen to make love to her there. The scene was about her feeling completely contaminated and not wanting to make love because she felt that way, but none of the words said that, nothing said that. So, it was our job to find a way to say that while saying all the other words. And Cher, who is enormously truthful, along with her talent, part of her talent is telling the truth. And you're halfway there assuming that's true of someone, she wants to serve and not be served, and it was very easy with Cher because she's immensely gifted.

Reba: You saw something in Cher and that changed her life.

Mike Nichols: Of course, there's nothing you can do for someone in movies if they can't do it themselves. It's not the camera doesn't lie. The camera does nothing but lie, I believe, because the camera is really only looking at something carefully selected, lit, and prepared. It's that at the same time the camera sees, I do believe, sees someone's nature. I think that what we love in the stars is their nature and that's what we see. And that's what nobody can fake. You have it or you don't. And the people who have gotten lucky and movies have found that in themselves. There's no way anybody else can do it. The luck has to be the part. It's all about getting the part that allows you to express certain parts of yourself. And these women were lucky. And I do like women. And it certainly helps if everybody's happy to be there.

Reba: So, what do you want audiences to take away from this film?

Mike Nichols: Well, I guess, I mean the main thing I want is what seems to be true is that they have a good time, is that they laugh. It's very funny. It's very pleasurable to make an audience laugh or to let an audience laugh. And then there's another thing of the picture which is to some extent it's about things that are gone, things that we don't have anymore: simple words, good guys and bad guys, nice girls and bad girls. What did you say? Foreplay?

Reba: I said romance.

Mike Nichols: Sorry, I'm terribly sorry. Well, in a way they are the same. I don't think that we've said goodbye to foreplay or romance, but everything is more complicated, and things actually were simpler. Tolstoy said, "People of a little imagination always think everything is happening for the first time," but some things are happening for the first time. The world is changing very fast. And I think some of the things that we miss, like simple words and good guys and bad guys, that it's nice to know that they were there and that they can still be there as part of our lives if they're not part of the greater world.

Reba: Has moviemaking changed?

Mike Nichols: You know what I think really has changed is that there was for a long time a thing among actors that to be difficult was glamorous. And it came from certain real models. You could see in movies like *A Star Is Born*. You can see Judy Garland saying, "Could you give me a minute?! Could you just leave me alone?!" And everybody thought that was the way to be, but that's all over now. It was a whole bunch of very good actors and they knew their job and they were ready and that showed up and they did their work and they had a good time and they played ball in between shots. And they have no problems and they give no problems. They love their lives and they love what they can do and they're very lucky. They're sort of the top of their generation. They're already very successful movie actresses, the bunch of them. And they know they're lucky and they have no complaints that have made for a very happy place and productive place.

Reba: It was happy because you made it that way.

Mike Nichols: My job was easy.

The VP of publicity, Reese, had given me films before she left. Her successor, Sally Van Slyke, was not thrilled to work with me, as she wanted to flex her own power and use her own people. I assumed she had to put up with me because I had material for five films that I had been hired for and was still working on. What I did not know was that Marvin Antonowsky was the reason I was still there. He insisted on keeping me there as long as he was president of marketing. When Marvin Antonowsky left the studio, his successor Ed Roginski also ensured my job while he was in charge. I had no idea that these two powerful allies were looking out for me. Both men were impressed with the television distribution network I had set up as no other vendor working on film publicity had ever thought to do it.

I let my ego get in the way when Sally told me not to cut a profile of Mike Nichols. Rather than doing what she asked I tried to persuade her to let me continue cutting the way I had before she took the job. Why fix it if it's not broken? The proven airplay my profile pieces were getting was sensational. My behavior, however, was atrocious; loaded with sugar, I acted like an over-the-top, angry alcoholic. I had a difficult time controlling my temper, so I covered my insecurity with bravado and bluster. I felt I knew everything about producing, distributing, and working with local stations when it came to video publicity since I had done it successfully for five years. In my defense, I knew what local television stations wanted and she only wanted programming that would please the producer of the films.

Sally was looking for an excuse to get rid of me and I gave it to her by insisting that my stations expected profiles. I felt a profile of Mike Nichols, the Academy Award winning director of *The Graduate* and director of *Biloxi Blues,* would give us the airplay that the other material could not do. I was surprised that after five successful years of producing video profiles she would not listen to me.

As soon as Ed Roginski died in 1988, with no one to protect me, I was fired.

The Nichols' interview has never seen the light of day until now. In fact, I never looked at it again after I was told not to cut it. What really surprised me was that I still had the master, not Universal.

I see how I sabotaged my own success. A big part of me was

so scared by the large sums of money I was being paid; I was sure they would find out I was not qualified. This was not a new fear, but one that developed once the money started rolling in. I was never scared when I had my television show that paid me $30,000 a year, but in my first year of this business I billed high six figures, and that terrified me. At any moment I felt sure they would realize their mistake and take the work away. To deal with this fear I turned to my drug of choice, chocolate-covered peanuts. I had really taken my success for granted because of the huge airplay my profiles were getting. It never dawned on me that my actions could cause me to lose jobs or even lose a major film studio. Especially one that had given me a lot of work based on my track record. But it was happening.

12
MICHAEL J. FOX

I struggled for a long time to get to Judi Schwam. I tried connecting with her when she was a VP at Columbia Pictures, but she already had a team she worked with. That was until Diane Keaton needed to be interviewed for *Baby Boom* after two companies had failed. Judi Schwam was now a senior VP at United Artists and was so pleased with the Keaton interview I did that she gave me another job: Michael J. Fox for the film *Bright Lights, Big City*. I delivered on Diane Keaton and I continue to deliver on the movie assignments she gave me.

To be honest, I don't know how I did this interview as I was filled with sugar, filled with fear, and filled with disgust that I could not stop eating. The interview was done in a hotel room in Beverly Hills, and along with Fox was his personal publicist, Nanci Ryder. I so wanted to impress his publicist that it took all the energy and concentration I could muster to get the interview done. I didn't want her to see me as a loose cannon, which was what I felt like inside. I wanted to please her with an interview that would sell the film and Michael J. Fox. I hoped that no one could tell what I was feeling and how grateful I was for the job after my failure at Universal.

The first thing that helped me on this interview was that Michael J. Fox remembered me from *Light of Day*. The studio only wanted a profile of Michael J. Fox even though the film starred Kiefer Sutherland, Phoebe Cates, and Micheal J. Fox's girlfriend Tracy Pollan from *Family Ties*—the two married shortly after this interview was done.

Reba: What did you use for cocaine?

Michael J. Fox: When we talk about the amount of drug use in the film, one should be very clear to point out that it was not drugs. I was having lunch at the pyramid commissary, and I saw Al Pacino, and when I could finally get my mouth to work and get coordinated and realized I wasn't going to be an idiot, I asked him what they used in Scarface, and he said lactose—lactate, maybe, just milk sugar. So, we use that. So the funny part about that is that you do it, and there's no sensation at all, but the next day, your nose a little clogged, and then around noon, it breaks and milk starts to run down your face. So, you're in the deli, you know, ordering a Reuben and milk is running out your nose. It's a little bizarre.

Reba: Why stop doing comedies?

Michael J. Fox: Everything about *Light of Day* indicated that it would not be successful in a lot of ways. For me, it wasn't a lead role. It was a very down subject. It was a very gritty film. It was a very gritty filmmaker, who I respected a lot, but he's not a guy who makes, you know, 101 Dalmatians or whatever; that's just not what he does. Going into it, there was no way this film could be a commercial success. But I almost wanted that, you know, people said, "You just made a film [Back to the Future] that made $200 million, what do you do to follow?" And I said, "I just do something that I did, I just try to find something that I really want to do that will appeal to me and not worry about the money." And I did, and I had a great time. I learned a lot. I changed in a lot of ways that I wanted to. I mature in a certain sense, both creatively and personally. I became a much better guitar player that I've ever been before. I met some great people. I have to think that the story about *Light of Day* and it always makes me laugh. And I was having dinner with my agent after *Light of Day* had come out. And he was telling me about the box office, which you've been disappointing. And he said, "You know, I don't want you to get upset." And I said, "I'm not upset." I said, "I never did *Light of Day* for it to be a big box office success. And he said, "Congratulations." [Laughs]

So, you know… So maybe I succeeded, who knows, maybe in failure, I succeeded. I do know that what was very funny, though, is that people saw the upside of it as me breaking out and doing something different and taking a risk. And they'd say, "Oh, it's great that you took a risk." And then *Secret of My Success* came out and it did good. And, and so when Newsweek or whoever says he doesn't take any chances, I said, "I took a chance; you hated it." But you know, that's life.

It all comes down to do what you really believe in, realize that what you want to do ultimately is to be able to look to the people you expect to come and see your work in the eye and say, "Listen, I'm doing the best I can do. And maybe what I'm doing is a little strange and off the beaten path but I'm believing in it. And I'm taking all the things that you always liked, and I'm applying it." And that's enough. I don't need a stamp of approval from the box office. And I don't need a stamp of approval from the critics, and I don't need the stamp of approval from other people in this community. I just need to know that I did what I thought was right, and I did it the best that I could do it. And that'll always be the ultimate goal. It doesn't hurt when it does well, you know, that's nice too, that validation is always good. The great thing about success, financial success in terms of box office for a film is that it perpetuates your career, that's all, that I get more shots. You know, they say for every hit, you get four tries. So, I'm back to now for new at bats then it's great. And so what do I do? I do *Bright Lights, Big City*, and I'm going to go do a movie about Vietnam. And then you know, my third bat I'll do, you know, Alex Keaton goes to Paris or something or *Back to the Future 2* we have coming up.

So that always exists. So, my agenda right now is to just do interesting films and try to satisfy myself in that I'm doing the best work that I can do, and I'm not hitting to, you know, left field every time. You know, I'm trying to balance a couple times, and you know, just doing it different.

Reba: You've had a phenomenal success as an actor as I'm sure you've noticed it.

Michael J. Fox: Yeah. I'm slightly aware.

Reba: What about the movie business? It's less of a grind.

Michael J. Fox: It's much less of a grind. I've done *Family Ties* for six years. And I'll be doing a seventh year, and I believe that'll be it—mutual consent between all the participants, I think, seven years, we're going to call it. It's been a great experience. My film career effectively started about the fourth season—maybe the third, I'm not quite sure. And I've been juggling both, which is made for twelve-month work years. And, you know, constantly, constantly working and shifting in and out. It's going to be nice after the show...I'm going to miss the show tremendously. It's the most fun I've ever had. And it changed my life. And I love all the people involved, it will be need to know that I can do two films a year and still have six months to rest or, you know, a couple of weeks to rest at very least between the things that I do. That's going to be great.

My future is, probably acting was going to be in films, if I'm permitted to, you know, if they'll let me, you know, it's not my ballroom so I can only say I want to dance; I can't say that I'm going to, you know, but I'm going to do that. And I also have a television production company at Paramount that will be producing television and feature films. So, I want to do that, too, and hopefully direct some point. I've been invited to and I could just if I can find the time. So, after the show, my life is going to open up and I'm going to have a lot more opportunities to pursue different.

Reba: How do you to find a time to have any kind of life?

Michael J. Fox: Well, you were mentioning Mike Nichols saying that life is a pendulum, you always have your highs and lows. And life is a pendulum in that you'll have a point in your life where you're relaxed and points your life where you're hectic. But that can always scale down and move into whatever your life is. So that my life and other people's life may be very hectic. For me, it's my life so I can find space in there that you know, fifteen minutes for you is the time waiting for a bus or someone else's time waiting for, you know, waiting for the paper to get there. Fifteen minutes to me is like great. And that fifteen minutes becomes five hours. I mean, it's great and I've just learned to use that time in my life so I'm very, very comfortable.

Reba: Did you consciously pick roles that are as far away from or is there Alex and Jamie...

Michael J. Fox: There's me and Alex, there's Alex in every character I play, there's every character I play in Alex too. I don't consciously try to do different things. My attention is caused by different things. When I read Bright Lights, I mean, I'd heard about Bright Lights for a long time. I had a conversation with Tom Cruise about Bright Lights when he was going to do it and he told me about it. And I read it, I liked it, I could never see myself playing it. I said, "You know, this is really neat. I hope someone makes it and does a good job of it." One day the phone rang and Sydney Pollack called and then saying that they'd like to talk to me about doing this. I read the book again and all of a sudden it all made sense. And I said, "Yeah, I could do this, and I can do it well and I could now."

I found a point of view in this piece that means something to me, which is that it's very much the story of a young man and the people that he loves in his sense of obligation to them. It's not a story about drugs and it's not a story about self-destructive behavior purely. And that all just happened. I went, and I talked to them, and a week later I was on the film. So that happens in my life. I was already to do, in this next hiatus, ready to do a comedy, *The Secret of My Success*, with somebody else and probably do very well, and I read this script that Brian De Palma sent me and involved going to go into Thailand for three months and like fighting off leeches, which is nobody's idea of a good time, but I love the story, so I'm going. I really operate in that way. There's no method to my madness; it's purely madness.

Reba: Would you do another TV series?

Michael J. Fox: At that point in my life that I did it, I would absolutely do it again and I would pray that I could be as lucky as I was that time.

At this point, no, I don't think so. I'm interested in producing a TV series and writing for it and in casting it in getting a great group of people together to do some interesting work. Acting in it at this point, I just need a rest, you know, ask me in a couple of years. It's been six, it will be seven, that's a lot of time. And I have—my constitution is not what it used to be. I'm not as tough as I was. But it's satisfying, and it's continually changing. And there are lows in the highs, and that's good, and it's not bad. It's something that is a happy coincidence to me, doing what I love to do. The fact that I'm successful at it, it's great.

Reba: I love your description of being an actor, and you broke it down in ninety percent is acting and five percent, and only five percent was money.

Michael J. Fox: Yeah, but that's enough. Well, money, you know, money changes your life, and it makes a lot of things possible. It's also a burden in some ways, but that's very easy for me to say. And, you know, I mean, there are, you know, farmers in Iowa that would love to have that burden, you know? But it really, it gets down to once you're eating and you can buy presents for your family at Christmas, and you get a roof over your head. It's just a way of keeping points. And the great part really—if there's any really great part of success, a successful acting career, it's being allowed to act, and being given a lot of options, a lot of choices, and being able to read the work of a lot of really good writers and figure out what you want to do. And that's the upside all the way.

Reba: Any regrets?

Michael J. Fox: No, no, I don't have any regrets at all. It's been great. It's been really terrific. And I enjoyed doing what I do, and I made mistakes. And there are things that have hurt, as we've all had things that have hurt us on our way, but you know, it's the Back to the Future theory, you know, you go back and move a pen, you know, the other side of a desk, and the whole world is gone when you get back, you know. I don't want to change anything; everything is great.

Reba: Since you're Irish, you're going to have the best answer. Do you believe in luck?

Michael J. Fox: Absolutely. I'm the luckiest guy on the planet. I'm like extremely lucky. I'm telling you—saying something extremely personal now but I want to say just because it's such a great story that I just purchased a farm. When I went to see it, I knew it was going to be the farm that I wanted because it's a couple hundred years old and the name that it was given when it was built was the Lottery Hill Farm. It was built by a guy who won a lottery in 1828 and then he took his lottery winnings and he bought this farm and I said, "Yeah, this is me. You know this is, like, some nouveau riche schmo won a lottery 175 years ago and, like, I'm going to live there now because that's who I am." I'm really a lucky guy. I went out fishing the other day... And I know some people don't believe in fishing, but I happen to like to fish and I went out. There are people that their whole lives try to catch marlin, can't catch it. Can't catch a marlin, can't even see a marlin. I went out the other morning and got two marlins. Got a 250-pound marlin, and a hundred-pound marlin. And it's like life. And the scary part about luck is that it can go away but the beauty of it is to realize you had it once and that was enough, you know?

Reba: In a way you parlay being short into the career. And the reason I'm asking is it last time you gave us an incredible statement and it's for the kids in America do terrible [inaudible] on themselves? Right? It's about, you know, you said to me last time you got to play the hand you're dealt with.

Michael J. Fox: Absolutely. Well, if you have a drug problem, stop doing drugs. If you overeat, stop overeating. If you are, you know, if you are abusive to people, stop doing it. If you're short, what you can do, stop being short? You just are what you are, you know, that's a physiological card that was dealt to that you can't do anything about, and I don't know so much that I parlayed being short into a good thing. It just never was ever...there was never the possibility of it being a seed for a bad thing. I mean, it just is, you know what I mean? You can and if you want to you can get into a whole, you know, takes less time behind my pants mentality and look at all the upside of it, but it just, it is what it is. You know, what's funny is my greatest satisfaction is actually reading a review and again, a critic not having anything nasty to say because the work was fairly solid, well, he's short. I was like, you bonehead.

Judi Schwam gave me another film right after Michael J. Fox's interview called *Rain Man,* which five years later got me an invitation to join the Academy of Motion Pictures Arts and Sciences. I am still a member and vote for the Oscars every year.

13
TOM CRUISE

I only interviewed Tom Cruise once and it was for the film *Rain Man* in 1988. I was hired to shoot behind the scenes, do on-set interviews, and produce a finished electronic press kit (EPK), which included a "making of" featurette. That's not what happened as Tom Cruise was famous enough to have the set closed because he kept blowing his lines.

I didn't know what to expect, and I was scared that I wouldn't be able to produce what United Artists hired me for because I didn't have any behind-the-scenes footage. That meant everything hinged on the interviews. I found Tom Cruise to be warm and charming. He did not hesitate in answering questions, and afterward I was relieved I had material for the video profile that would get the most exposure.

Reba: Did Dustin get you involved?

Tom Cruise: I met Dustin before, when I went backstage at *Death of a Salesman* and he was just very generous to me. I went out to dinner with him and Lisa and his family and everything. And he sent me a couple of books, stuff that he was developing and said let's work together. And then I got a call from him and he told me that he was going to send the script of *Rain Man* over and he was interested to hear what I had to say, and he'd like me to do it with him. I thought it was a great role. You could just tell it was a skeleton of something really terrific. And I got really excited about it, and then we started working on it.

Reba: When you say you started working, you put input into scripts?

Tom Cruise: Well, with this film, especially when you get to more complex characters and you put so much into it, you work on anything as soon as you get the script, it's always adjusting. And once you really start doing a lot of research and working on the characters, things change.

Reba: When you finished the film, I bet you really felt good about it.

Tom Cruise: I mean, what rubbed off was the work in terms of the learning process, and every film I do is just that. You get new tools to work with and different things to really experiment with and try things and see what works and see what's not going to work and I mean, working with Hoffman and Levinson. I mean, Hoffman, first of all, is such a tremendous actor—unbelievable. And I just learned a lot from him and working with him I really got to play around with stuff, and it allowed me a lot of freedom artistically. I mean, that's kind of thing that I sit back and look at when you're going into the next film, what can I take with me from this one and from everything? I think it's a kind of a build on what I've really focused on in my career is with each picture, I want to try something new, try something different, try to use the things that in the last one and not necessarily doing the same thing and trying different tools in a different way, and that way you walk away feeling different. I mean, from a project like this I can't say that the role changed me; playing Charlie has really enlightened me in other areas in as much as my work.

Reba: Was there a fear that you were going to be typecast?

Tom Cruise: No, not really. When *Risky Business* came out, that's all the scripts I was being offered was all Joel Goodson. And then I did something completely different, All the Right Moves, or it would have been an easy thing for me to get typecast.

Reba: But I think at this point in your career, you don't have to worry about being typecast. Do you agree?

Tom Cruise: I don't think at any point in my career I had any problem with being typecast. People tend to want to put everyone in a category so that they can understand it and somehow come to terms with it. And I think that that's always a struggle in looking for myself for different things. Yeah, I think it's always a struggle and difficult to find something good and to find something different that you never played before. It's always going to be a challenge.

Reba: Did you always want to act?

Tom Cruise: I think somewhere I did. Yes, I did. In growing up I was involved in creative drama in different schools as we moved a lot, and I went to fifteen different schools. It was in the late sixties, early seventies, when creative drama was movement to music. You know, you moved to Bob Dylan and do these kinds of abstract poems, these little play houses and stuff. And then I wasn't involved in theater for about five years. And then I did a play in high school and just really enjoyed it again. And then I know from then on that's what I wanted to do.

Reba: When did you decide you wanted to be an actor?

Tom Cruise: Well, the thing is, I really didn't even think of making a living being an actor, I just wanted to be an actor. I never thought, if someone told me, "Oh, yeah, sure, you'll be working with Dustin Hoffman nine years from now," I wouldn't have believed it. And going to my mother and telling her that I'm going to be an actor wasn't really a difficult thing. I mean, just in the way our family is, it's whatever you want to do, what's going to make you happy, you know? And we didn't have a lot of money and any education. We had to pay for ourselves. And so once you turn seventeen, eighteen, you're free to go on to live your life and finish high school and pursue your dream, whatever it may be.

Reba: Was it scary?

Tom Cruise: I really wasn't scared. I must have been nuts, you know? And I just...I don't know, I just had this thought it was going to be tremendous adventure, and that's kind of the way it was.

Reba: Are you good at auditions?

Tom Cruise: I don't think I was particularly good at auditions. Some of them, I was really bad, so I feel for actors even now when going through the casting process and they come in and read. It's very difficult when everyone says, "Look, don't give us a performance, we just want to see?" But they're looking for a performance, and you can't really show your stuff as an actor and how you're going to play the role and develop it until you really get in there. And then I just went in and I just started saying, "Look, I didn't think of it in terms of auditions. I thought of it in terms of when I'm in that room, I'm a working actor and that role is mine for that fifteen minutes. That role is mine and I'm going to play it and I'm going to play it as many different ways as if we were shooting it or I was on stage playing the role through rehearsal and I'm going to try it fifteen different ways to make them sit there and listen to it," which, you upset some people. And sometimes it worked and sometimes it didn't work. But I enjoyed it.

Reba: What was it like when you first filmed?

Tom Cruise: Oh, I jumped. I remember when I got *Taps*, I was like jumping up and down. I was in New York, and I didn't have money to…I'd been living in New York, I guess a year and a half or something and I was just broke. I'd lost my job busing tables a couple of weeks before and I was looking for another job. I was unloading trucks at this place and I got laid off there and so I went to see my family for the weekend. I hitchhiked from New York City and at this time they were living in Jersey, so I hitchhiked into Jersey. And I had just walked out of the audition for *Taps*, and I just thought, well, I'm broke. If I get it, I get it, and if I don't, I'll just move on. But I really felt that I was right or this. And I remember walking up the driveway and my mother ooked through the curtains and she was on the phone and she's kind of a little excited. So, I walked in the back of the house and she's just kind of holding her breath and she said, "There's a phone call for you." That's kind of how she said it. And I got on the phone and, you know, they said, "Look, you're going to be doing this film *Taps* and it's nine weeks of work," or something like that, "and you're going to get paid $850 a week." And I just couldn't believe it. I just put down the phone, jumping up and down. Then I went through—I remember reading the script because before that I only read a few scenes. "Bullshit, bullshit. My part. My part. Bullshit, bullshit, bullshit. My part." And just went through the whole script like that. And it was wonderful and exciting. I was ecstatic.

Reba: How did you deal with the rejection?

Tom Cruise: Oh, I was rejected a lot growing up. I was always the new kid. There was a time in my life when it had been a great adventure in moving, that's the way I looked at it. I love moving. It's hard for me to stay in one place. And going to new places, there was constant rejection, constant rejection when I was growing up. I was not a great athlete, you know, I wrestle but I was not a great athlete. I worked very hard at everything I did, but I was never great at any one sport. I mean, hockey was my best sport. I just was always in the formative stages and then we'd move. And the same scholastically, the education that I had, I'd start getting a rhythm in the class and then we'd move.

So, it was a lot of adapting to different situations and a lot of frustration. And auditioning for me, I took on the attitude you're either going to get eaten alive by the system that you're in or you're going to rise above it. And ever since I was very young, that's how I always felt about it and always strive for to just make the best out of a situation. It's not rejection because in every situation there is a lesson to be learned and there's something that you can move forward on. And audition for me, you know, I was a working actor. I didn't just take that as an audition, I took it that I am working now, I am a working actor, and I'm going to play this role. The whole thing is, I mean, when you're making a film or you're doing something, you've got to, you know, you're doing a play or anything, you've got to get up there and really show yourself and play around and do things that you can't be afraid to be humiliated and you can't look at it in those terms. So, auditioning for me, I didn't take it in terms of rejection.

Reba: Where did the discipline come from to be an actor?

Tom Cruise: When I love something, I was really…I wasn't the most responsible person growing up. I was never a…really great in school. But I found that when I really love something that I just went after it ferociously, and I think I know that's how I felt about acting.

Reba: It was easy because that's what you wanted to do.

Tom Cruise: Well, and also the problem that I had with school is that compounded with dyslexia. I didn't have a good education because I was never in a place—when something is being taught, I'd always come in the middle of the year, in the middle of the class, and I was either behind or ahead or never starting from the basics and working my way through the course. It was always in the middle of it. And I was always kind of having to catch up or just try to make something work. I didn't have the full understanding of the course. And that was a lot of the problem with my education. I mean, in thinking about it and looking back on why reading so difficult. And then, because I'm not an extreme dyslexic, I mean, my little sister had, was just a hundred times worse than me. But I am dyslexic, but that compounded with not understanding fully the course. I found that very difficult.

Reba: Do you read well now?

Tom Cruise: Oh, I do. I do find if I'm reading something like anyone, something that's interesting, I'll read it, you know I can't put it down, and, but if something is tedious, it's just a battle for me to get through. But that's not unusual to anyone.

Reba: Why car racing? Doesn't the speed scare you?

Tom Cruise: The speed scares me not at all. People always say, well, how fast do you go? You don't really even think in terms of it's a rush, you know, going down the straightaway or in a corner. If you're going into a bank corner and you've got your foot to the floor and you're going 130 miles an hour, 140 miles an hour, it's exciting. It's really exciting. I enjoy that. But there's a lot more to racing than just goingfast. You really mentally have to be very disciplined and know the game inside and out because you don't want to make a lot of mistakes

Reba: You can interchange racing with acting. It's timing, judgment, mental discipline, and patience.

Tom Cruise: Yes, you can identify racing with acting. I mean, there are many parallels: the discipline. And interestingly enough, the patience, even at the high speeds and in passing and you really have to be patient. You really have to be disciplined. There's a lot of timing involved, and you have to be really on top of your game.

Reba: Is success everything you thought it was going to be?

Tom Cruise: It's much more, actually. I mean, in terms of success, I always think how do you define success for one person? You always hear, "Oh, don't change when you become successful. So many people have changed, and they don't know how to handle success." And I don't think that people change when they become successful. Who they are becomes more magnified because there's a lot of pressures and there's a tremendous amount of responsibility, tremendous amount of power, and you really have to take responsibility for, you have to grow and really address all of that. And the politics…I always say, "God, if I ever became successful, I wouldn't have to deal with the politics within the situation, then everyone, it would be much easier." But it's actually, I enjoy it. I want to be successful, and I enjoy the responsibility and the pressure. And the thing that happens with a lot of people as they become afraid to grow and they stop challenging themselves and kind of go for what got them there. And that's really what I've always focused on and not stopping.

Reba: You're not afraid of pressure?

Tom Cruise: No, I love pressure.

Reba: Even exams?

Tom Cruise: I don't like taking exams, but I don't mind pressure.

Reba: You're also not afraid to take risks with your roles. Where do you think that comes from?

Tom Cruise: Well, I don't really—I think I'm afraid to lose everything that I've gained. I get paid a lot of money, but it's not important to me.

Reba: I don't think this was a money question. I get the feeling that there's an edge of excitement in taking the risk.

Tom Cruise: Taking a risk makes me want to get up in the morning. You say to yourself, "God, I don't know if I can do it. I hope I can." I want that excitement. I want to get up in the morning and feel that excitement, those butterflies, and know that I'm not doing the same thing.

His publicist at the time was Andrea Jaffe and she was quite famous and very powerful. For Cruise's video profile interview, I had to actually create a full script before it could be edited. The footage and Tom's interview had to be approved by not only Andrea but seventeen other people. The only name not on the list was Tom Cruise.

When I got back our script from her, it was like a test paper with a D in red on it saying that this looked like the crap on *Entertainment Tonight*. I was thrilled as my job was to disguise a paid commercial to look like a Barbara Walters/Oprah–style interview. Publicists are really smart when it comes to protecting their clients, but when a soft interview that does not place the client in a precarious position cannot get approved, you know there is a problem. To be honest, I have no idea who went over Andrea's head to get us the approval to send out the three-minute video profile for the film, but this interview was really well received on my 120 US stations. The film went on to earn over 350 million dollars—unheard of for a small drama at the time—and earned Tom the best reviews of his career.

A postscript to this film—all the people involved went on to great success: The producer, Mark Johnson, took the Oscar for best picture. The Oscar for Best Actor went to Dustin Hoffman and the Oscar for Best Director went to the film's Barry Levinson. The executive producers, Peter Guber and Jon Peters, went on to become the chairmen of Sony Pictures Entertainment the next year. If that was not enough, later the film won a Golden Bear, the German Oscar. The Motion Picture Academy looks fondly on Oscar-winning films, and I do believe that's what got me the invitation to join.

No one outside of the film community knew what I was doing until I got a call from a reporter at the *Washington Post* wanting to know why the Tom Cruise interviews, which she had seen in Philadelphia and in the District of Columbia, were the same except for the narrator. What made the profiles work was each station used their anchor to voice over my voice and keep it local. Busted! I told her I was going into a meeting, everyone in Hollywood uses that line, and I would call her back—which I did after I got approval to talk about what I had been doing for five years. She wrote a story about my video profiles and her story gave me a passing grade. Interestingly, that story did not get me any new business, so maybe I was still a secret in Hollywood.

14

MICHAEL CAINE

Without a doubt Michael Caine is a charming man, and he surprised me by telling stories I had not found in my research. If you asked the right personal questions, Michael Caine would give you very candid answers, which was not normally done on publicity interviews. I wasn't like anybody else in my field because I wanted to know what made these people tick, and the only way to find out was to ask. I'm surprised that any studio or production company ever hired me, as my questions tended to get personal. I knew the reason I was in demand was simple: I got a lot of television airplay. In my twenty-three years of working in Hollywood, not one publicist ever stopped my interviews.

Michael Caine was a product of the movie-star system. They changed his name from Maurice Joseph Micklewhite Jr. and even tried to change his accent, which was Cockney. His generation of name-changed actors included Rock Hudson, Tab Hunter, and even Anne Bancroft. Only a decade later most actors got to keep their given names like Gene Hackman, Dustin Hoffman, and Paul Newman. The interview was conducted during a long shooting break, and Caine seemed like he enjoyed talking—and let's face it, I loved listening. The film tells the story of a man overlooked for a promotion and what he does to get to the top of the company. It was a very clever comedy about murder. It always helped when I liked a film that I was working on, which didn't happen all the time, but when it did it was magic.

Reba: Let's go all the way back first before we talk a little bit about the film. When did you know you wanted to be an actor?

Michael Caine: When I was ten years old, I was in a pantomime Cinderella in school, and I was voted the most popular actor in the show and I was given five shillings, 50 cents as a prize because I made everyone laugh. But what I actually had done is I'd gone on with my fly buttons open. And, so, what I did is I went into show business, but ever since then I've always checked my fly before I go on anywhere; I did it just now just before you started the camera. It was all there for me, laughter, money, applause, cheers, all in the one thing, and absolutely nothing to do with talent or anything whatsoever. So, I've tried to keep that going.

Reba: You probably never wanted to go into the fish business, did you?

Michael Caine: I certainly didn't. My entire family worked sort of in the fish market in London and it was very difficult to get into. It was really a nepotism city because it was a very good job, very high paying for someone who was unskilled in anything. But from my experiences at school, as I was an amateur dramatic society actor for many years, and I decided to become a professional one.

Reba: Well, before you became a professional, let's do the story about the book.

Michael Caine: I found a book in the library, which is called Teach Yourself Film Acting. So, I read this book and one of the things which stuck in my mind was "don't blink. You must never blink." So, for the next eight years, I walked around trying not to blink. The thing was, people around me, my mother and everybody, thought I had gone nuts. They thought I was a psychopath or so because every time they spoke to me, I used to frighten the life out of people. And at school they called me snake eyes, but I was determined not to blink. And what happens now if you see me in any movie on a take, I never blink. And that was the first thing I learned.

The other thing was to choose an eye, one eye, because otherwise you're looking at people, you look slightly bombed out of your mind if you're trying to look at the two eyes. I'm talking to you.

I put this eye to your left eye, which is closest to the camera. So that brings my face round at the camera. I get a much more concentrated thing if I just choose an eye and don't blink and keep looking at you. And that's what I do when I'm working.

Reba: You're funny.

Michael Caine: I was always kind of funny. My mother told me I was funny even before I knew I was funny. She told me this story of when I was two, we went to see her sister, my Auntie Lil, who was pregnant. And I asked my mother why she had such a fat stomach. My mother didn't want to go in with a two-year-old through the intricacies of pregnancy and they had just painted the kitchen and there was a smell of paint. And so she said very quickly—my mother's very quick, "She's got paint poisoning from the smell of this paint in the kitchen and her stomach has swollen up." So I said, "Well, fine." I accepted that. And my mother told me this story. She said we were going home on the bus and a pregnant woman got on and I asked her if she'd been painting the kitchen. So, I've always been funny sometimes without even knowing I'm funny. But I've always said funny stuff to people.

Reba: You set a tone on the film set. Are you even aware of it?

Michael Caine: Not really. What I am doing is—it's not entirely altruistic. I can't work in a tense atmosphere. So, if it starts getting tense, I'll break it with some dumb thing that I'll do, something dumb or funny or something that I think is funny or say something I think is funny and calm it all down. Because this was a very nerve-racking business and so I make a genuine effort to be friendly for the time that I'm working with anyone.

Reba: Well, it certainly shows.

Michael Caine: Well, I think this is my sixty-sixth film, and I've been doing it for thirty years, so I know a little bit about it. I put all my heart and soul into the first take, but it doesn't make sure I can't do take twelve, I don't have to work up to it. When I was training as an actor, one of the most important things that was said to me from a very famous woman producer I was working with, Joan Littlewood said to me, "The rehearsal is the work. The performance is the relaxation." So, when, by the time I get here to film a sequence, I have done all the work and the sweating at home so you've got this very calm exterior. I mean, it's really me talking to you. You're the actress and I'm supposed to be a certain person. If you can see it working, then we're not getting it right. You should see two people. And so now we've got to get it right down to small, infinitesimal, subtle. That's what I love about movie acting.

Reba: You're right because acting is supposed to be seamless.

Michael Caine: It's behavior, you see. Movie is behavior and reaction. The greatest compliment ever given to me as an actor in movies was when John Huston said to me, "You're one of the best listeners I've ever come across," which is what movie acting is. I listened to what you say and then I have an emotion about it and I think of an answer. That's behavior, but we call it movie acting, which is one of the most difficult things to do. And it's a bit self-defeating because the better you do it, the easier you make it look. And everybody says I've played everything from sadistic Nazis to homosexual transvestites. And I very often get reviews to say I played myself. I just have to worry about what I look like sometimes.

Reba: You play a lovable rogue. **Michael Caine:** A lovable rogue, yeah. Those are my favorite characters. The world is full of them. And the movie industry and world are chock full of them. You have to watch out for them. I'm lovable, but I'm certainly not a rogue, but you always like to be what you're not. It's vicarious, you know. I like going out and being a bit of a tough guy and I'm not, I'm very gentle soul, really. But I play the most dreadful characters, and I'm not a bit like any of them really. I like to cover it all up. I really am rather boring. I'm a very, very sort of stolid family man who would rather be at home with his family than actually do anything else. And I do gardening and I do cooking, and you've got me, "I thought he was supposed to be interesting." The only thing is I never talk about me or acting, I talk about them and who they are so they say I'm a very good conversationalist.

Reba: You're a great storyteller.

Michael Caine: Yeah. I tell stories. And of course with my life, if you think of the life I've had, I know lots of stories, but some of them are so outlandish. I never tell them because people say, "Oh, my God, you know, actors, they exaggerate and I'm sure he's lying." A lot of stories I never tell people because they wouldn't believe them anyway. I mean, my whole life you wouldn't believe anyway. I was doing a picture with Sly Stallone, directed by John Huston, and Sly kept saying to me, he said, "John never says anything to me about what I should do." I said, "He never says anything to me." He says, "I'm going to talk to him about this." I said, "You ask him?" So Sly says, "John?" He says, "You never give me any direction." And John said, "The first talent for director is to cast." He said, "I've cast you right. I don't have to tell you anything." He said, "If I was a bad director, I'd be telling you all day to do what I wanted. You do what I want without me asking." And that was it. And that's what he does.

Reba: I think you have that little boy charm we first saw in *Alfie*.

Michael Caine: Possibly there is. What happened to me was, when I was growing up, my father was in the war in World War II and so he was away for six years and I was brought up by my mother on her own with my brother. And she said, instead of, "God, I've got to look after you on my own." She went the other way, says, "Your father is away. Now you've got to look after me." And I am responsible, but it's like being responsible toward a mother, which is where the little boy comes in and it works. I always remember when I first went to France and was speaking French for the first time, all the girls were sort of wilting because it was like this great, big, grown man, and he's talking like a little boy, and they used to melt right in front of me, the French girls. It was great, and all the girls would go, "Oh, God." And it's this little boy quality, which I am not unaware of, and I've used quite viciously through my life.

Reba: You're very calm.

Michael Caine: A lot of it has to do with a man call James Clavell. I used to be very, very highly strung, and I was working with him, who was directing me in a film, and I lost my temper over something. Now James Clavell had been taken prisoner when he was fifteen by the Japanese, and the way he survived the five or six years as a prisoner, he told me, was he became a Japanese and think like they did and that's how he survived mentally. And he broke the set for an hour, took me around the corner after my outburst and talked to me about face and losing face. And I've never lost my temper in a work situation, so if I lose it at was at home because I don't have any face at home. They all laugh at me anyway. But in a work situation you could lose face, so I don't lose my temper. If you think in terms of the actual phrase "losing face," that means that someone else has won.

Reba: If you weren't making films, what would you like to do?

Michael Caine: I'd be a writer. That's it. The great thing about writing is that you don't have to go out. I love to stay home. And the other thing is if you want to go anywhere, you can pick somewhere you like to write about and then you write it off. So, I think that's an ideal situation. You go where you like for writing or you stay at home. And of course, you don't have to look your best. You don't have to shave in the morning. In fact, I have a contract to write my autobiography with Random House.

Reba: Will you kiss and tell?

Michael Caine: No, I won't kiss and tell. It's more of the flavor, it's supposed to be funny, put it that way. But no, not kiss and tell because I hate that when they kiss and tell and I'm in it. I have a wife and two daughters; I think that side of my life is irrelevant now that I've been happily married for eighteen years.

Reba: You delivered all kinds of characters and yet whenever people talk about you, you're always the sexy scoundrel that women love.

Michael Caine: Yeah, they do because of Alfie. Alfie was based on my best friend. It wasn't me. He got all the girls. I didn't. His name was Jimmy Buckley. He was a cockney boy. And he was kind of better looking than me. And he got all the girls. I used to get the leftovers. It's like George Burns said, he said, "What was your worst woman you ever had?" I said, "Terrific."

Reba: In looking back on your career, do you have any regrets?

Michael Caine: No. I started out my life where the one firm principle was that I was not going to regret the things I did when I'm six-ty- five and sitting on the porch in my rocking chair. I'll be sitting there regretting things I didn't do. I think to be old and regretting things you didn't do is the most dreadful thing. I will sit there and regret a lot of things I did, but nothing I didn't do.

Reba: And is fame everything you thought it was going to be?

Michael Caine: Yes. I think fame is an extraordinary thing. I mean there are things I don't like about fame, but the thing that I liked most about fame, I'm at home everywhere with everybody because no one is suspicious of me. I mean, I could walk up to a woman in the street on a dark night in a lonely alleyway, anyone else she would run or scream, but she would just think that he's not the Boston Strangler or Jack the Ripper.

And so, no one is suspicious of me. Also, with fame, every-body sort of trusts you. And when I walked through the streets in New York, everybody says, "Hi, Mike, how's it going?" "Right, I'm fine." And I'm at home everywhere and I always get good tables in restaurants, but that's because I'm a famous restauranteur, not because I'm a famous actor.

Reba: You have this effect on women of all ages that we feel safe.

Michael Caine: We've got back to my mother. You see, it's growing up with a woman all the time. So, I understand and know wom-en. I mean, as a little boy, I knew I had to figure out when to ask for some candy or ask for something and when to keep out of the way. So, I've made it very close study of this one woman all my life, which means I know all women react to certain things. And I think you get a lot of that with boys who are brought up by a woman.

Reba: Can I ask one more story about your mother and the premier of *Zulu* when she stood outside? Is that true?

Michael Caine: That's typical of my mother. It was my first big movie, for a film called *Zulu*, premiered in London. And I said to her, "Look, I haven't got a girlfriend who I want to take to this. I'll hire an evening dress and a fur coat, and you'd be my date for the night." And she said no. And I tried for a month to talk her into it. She said, "No way, I don't want to go." So, I got a girlfriend and I took her to the premiere and the crowd were shouting and screaming with lots of flash bulbs and the police holding the crowd back. And as I was going through and posing and saying, "Hello, hello," I looked in the crowd and there being pushed back by the police was my mother. She had come all this way on the bus. It was miles on the bus just to see me walk in. But she wouldn't come in with me. Typical. I think it's typical of her. I think it's typical of mothers.

Reba: She did enjoy your success?

Michael Caine: Oh, tremendously. Yes, she never mentions it when I'm there, but the minute I've gone, everybody knows instantly whose mother she is, believe me.

After Michael told the story of his mother standing behind the police line to watch him walk into his first film premiere, I told him it sounded like my mother, who never let me know how proud she was of me, but let everybody know who her daughter was and what I was doing. It seems our mothers came from the same place no matter where in the world they lived. To this day no matter how many stars I've interviewed, Michael Caine remains one of my favorites.

When I went to New York for the film *A Shock to the System* in early 1989 I was so sure I would be able to turn around my company because I expected to get more films. I stopped working to be with my mother during her last seven months of life in 1988. Up until that year, I had been working on about fifteen films a year, but most of 1988 passed without me getting any work. I knew I would have to make a decision about my company.

15
DOWN THE AMAZON
AND UP TO THE TOP OF RUSSIA

Out of the blue, I got a phone call from Finland in 1989 offering me a film in the jungles of Brazil—my only new job after Michael Caine. What an adventure. I took the job, which included my husband, as I had no other new work. Just getting there was quite a challenge. It took three planes, each one smaller than the previous and I was bringing my own equipment as well as additional sound gear for the production company.

First, we flew to Manaus on a large plane and next we went to Boa Vista in the morning on a 737 so we could be picked up by the private plane that was to take us to the film set. Boa Vista is on a tributary of the Amazon. Our final plane that would take us to the location was the stunt plane used in the film. I was relieved when they told us that the bullet holes had been applied for the film and not to worry about them. That turned out to be the least of our worries, as the plane only had two seats—one for the pilot and one for an actor joining the film. My husband and I had to sit on the sound equipment in the cargo section. We flew over the rain forest, which was at times breathtaking and others totally obscured by smoke as they were burning it. The film was called *Amazon* and it starred Rae Dawn Chong, villain extraordinaire Robert Davis, and Kari Väänänen, Finland's biggest star.

The setting and story for the film took place on the banks of a tributary of the Amazon River where natives mined for diamonds. In fact, the village where we stayed did exactly what they did in the film, they mined for diamonds. Another interesting thing about this village was it had no roads and the only way to get in or out was by plane, and it had to be a small plane.

The production company built a small village within the village where we had a large kitchen, bathroom facilities, showers, and tent bedrooms with mosquito netting. Bathrooms were nonexistent prior to our arrival. The villagers used a hole in the ground. An image that really hit me hard was when I saw stacks of small coffins one on top of the other in the village carpenter's hut. Life in this village was very difficult. There was no sanitation and no medical care. The miners worked for The Company and when they got paid, they went to The Company store, bought the local liquor, and drank until they passed out and did it all over again the next day. It was like the company owned them.

We were quite a distraction from this daily grind. The production crew would hang out and drink and eat with the village miners. It was very different from any other location film set I had worked on. The isolation of the Amazon film set really forged a family unit among the cast and crew. It was nice to be included.

I found out later that the production company left the village all the buildings they had built and went on to build a school too. As difficult as this shoot was because of how primitive it was, I really loved being there and was grateful that I got to go.

By the time I got back from the Amazon, the sugar had totally taken over, and I was depressed and unable to make phone calls to get work on upcoming films.

This film shoot changed my life. I met a woman who introduced me to the twelve-step program for food—I never knew such a thing existed. She was the unit publicist. She told me all about the program that helped her find a way to live, that allowed her to lose the weight and get her life back on track. Her honesty allowed me open up about my compulsive eating and how I had stopped looking for new films, stopped networking, and only thought about food. Her empathy was empowering. She understood the pain of an eating disorder. I went to my first meeting on December 17, 1989, two weeks after I returned from the film shoot.

Six months after joining the twelve-step program, I had lost most of the excess weight and was able to return my focus to things other than food. Prior to achieving this clarity, I had made some very poor decisions. I had sold all my equipment because I would not need it. I cut my expenses as I was sure I was once again finished. But that was not the case.

Later in the year, I got a call from one of the producers of an independent film going into production in Russia called *The Ice Runner*. He wanted me to go to Russia, shoot behind the scenes, and conduct the interviews with the stars, Timothy Bottoms and Pat Morita. When the film got a distributor, I would be paid to finish the EPK. I would not be paid for my work up front, just my expenses. With nothing coming in, I thought this would look good on IMDB—the International Movie Data Base.

Once I knew I was going to Russia, I realized I had an opportunity to pick up more work as 20th Century Fox was shooting *Back in the USSR*. I saw listed in the trades that it would be shooting at Moss Studios, the biggest and oldest film studio in Moscow. I called the production company and offered to shoot some behind-the-scenes footage for free, which I knew I could sell when I got back. The offer was quickly accepted, and they sent me the script and the contact info for the producer and unit publicist. The trip turned out to be more interesting than I ever expected, starting with getting to Russia—specifically to Moscow. We flew Finnair and on our flight there were beauty queens from all over the world going to participate in a beauty pageant in Moscow. I was traveling with my husband and hiring a local crew from Russia to shoot for me. The only thing I had to bring were seven boxes of video tapes for them to use. It never dawned on me that this could be a problem going through customs.

Our flight arrived about eleven o'clock in the evening and every one of those beauty queens made sure they had their full makeup on. They deplaned carrying their ball gowns and wearing their crowns. They were quite a beautiful sight to behold. As we exited the plane and went down to the tarmac, there was a military jeep supporting a rather large machine gun turret mounted in the center manned by a non-smiling uniformed soldier.

Once inside the airport we found ourselves in a fairly large square gray room. The entire room was devoid of any conversation other than the faceless person in the security enclosure requesting identity papers and the guard directing the passengers to baggage inspection. There was no small talk; we were clearly not in Disneyland.

After our passports were checked, we were waltzed through customs with my seven boxes of video tapes. I found out how lucky we were when another camera crew that I knew from Paris came two days later and had *all* their equipment and videotapes held in customs. Russia was like the wild west at the time. The Berlin wall had come down the year before and the Russian mafia had moved in. The best food was on the black market. In fact, it seemed like everything was from the black market. We were staying in a hotel not intended for foreigners and it was not like any place we had ever stayed. The room had wires sticking out of the wall where the telephone would be connected but there was no switchboard, so I needed to get a working phone. I traded for a working phone with two packs of Marlboro cigarettes and some Tootsie Rolls. After two days of shooting in Moscow, we were off to our film *The Ice Runner* at the top of Russia in Arkhangelsk. First, my husband and I were shown to an empty gray boarding room and sat there until a woman wearing a babushka gestured for us to follow her. She led us to the tarmac of an Aeroflot plane, and she proceeded to push us up the steps and elbow people out of the way for us. Then she pulled a person out of their seat so I could sit with my husband, all of this without ever speaking a word to us. The man I sat next to was covered in a floor-length sable coat and very impressive matching hat, but I don't think he ever took a bath. During the flight the stewardesses came around selling nail polish, necklaces, and small plastic toys. Once we landed, we were not allowed to leave our seats until the crew deplaned before us.

Little did I know that the money for this film was being provided by the Russian mafia, and the man sitting next to me on the plane was one of the producers of the film. The setting for the film was in Arkhangelsk, which was famous for its secret submarine base and had only recently been opened to foreigners. The hotel we stayed at was very nice because it was created for the officers and crew of their submarine fleet. We shot by natural light only, so the shooting day was over by 1:00 p.m. Unlike the Fox film, which had bathrooms and great craft services, our film had no bathrooms, so the men used any space and the women tried to find a tree—there was a lot of yellow snow. I hired a local film student to shoot for me and paid him sixty dollars a day plus cigarettes and Tootsie Rolls. I must admit his footage was really terrific.

When our plane took off from Moscow, there was silence until the captain came on the intercom and announced that we were now out of Soviet airspace. The entire planeload of people broke out into loud and long applause. Obviously, we were not alone in the sense of oppressiveness of the authoritarian regime that we had just left behind. I found out later that they shot without ever looking at dailies to save money. Unfortunately, they never checked the gate to see if the camera was recording. It had frozen so there was no film footage from that time, only my video footage. I still have that footage of the film, as nothing else survived. They went back the next year in the spring and reshot the film, but none of the people involved in that first film ever came back, and I don't know what happened to that film.

The situation in my company was a well-kept secret except to my husband, and we decided that we were not going to put any money into the company to keep it going. I had very few films to finish and knew that I needed at least ten more to keep my company open and had no idea where the work would come from.

My answering machine was blinking after I returned from Russia, and when I heard the message from Teri Ritzer, I cried. After cleaning up my act from my eating disorder, I was much calmer and definitely thinner. I was more comfortable with myself. I had first met Teri Ritzer when she was a junior publicist at Universal assigned to oversee an interview I did with Tom Hanks for *The Money Pit*. We stayed in touch throughout her career changes—first as the editor for the *Hollywood Reporter* and then she became a vice president at 20th Century Fox International. She wanted me to re-edit the publicity materials that the studio had used to promote the film *For the Boys* in the states and replicate the profile style she had seen me do at Universal for the international market. My video profiles would play outside of the United States in sixty countries.

These two international films changed my life. The Amazon film got me into a twelve-step program, and the trip to Russia that I thought was my last hurrah turned out to be a second chance.

16
BRANDON LEE

After I produced my first profiles for For the Boys with Bette Midler and James Cann, I knew this was where I belonged. Those profiles got the most airplay that Fox international had ever had. I got to work good hours, usually only three hours compared to the fourteen to sixteen hours on domestic film sets as I was used to. I was fifty-six years old and knew that this was the right move for me. There was one more bonus working on films for international release—I did not have to deliver the tapes nor produce records of airplay from my television network anymore, the studio did that.

Teri Ritzer was so impressed with my work that she hired my company for a second film. And the film jobs kept coming for the next fifteen years no matter where she worked.

One of the movies Fox gave me was *Rapid Fire* starring Brandon Lee. It really excited me that I was going to meet the son of one of the world's greatest action-hero movie stars, Bruce Lee. I was to follow Brandon Lee around for a day with a video crew to film behind-the- scenes footage and then conduct an interview. For this interview, I only had the script to work with as the film was not finished being edited. Without any production notes, I had to rely heavily on my search because it wasn't enough to know that he was Bruce Lee's son I needed to figure out who he was. I wasn't surprised to learn that he was taught kung fu and given acting lessons at an early age, as I'm sure his father wanted him to follow in the family business.

Reba: When you're given a script with martial arts scenes, can you visualize how the action scenes are going to go?

Brandon Lee: I take the script and throw it out the window, as far as I'm concerned and you start from zero as a choreographer and you have the characters express things about themselves through the choreography that you're going to create. Fight choreography fascinates me, it's just wonderful. I used to watch my dad's films all the time, watch his choreography. He had beats and he'd have comedy beats, he'd have pauses to allow the audience to catch up. And I can see where he drew from; he drew from the old samurai films, and it's a rich tradition and it's one that hasn't been explored in America that much.

Reba: What do you draw from?

Brandon Lee: Well, you draw from your imagination. In terms of people who are out working right now, Jackie Chan, who is a martial artist and an actor and a director in Hong Kong, I think he's fantastic. His work is great. And then you draw from the martial arts, you draw from reality, you draw from your own experiences, your experiences in the gym, your experiences with what would happen. You ask yourself, if someone did this to me, what would I do, and then maybe you also try and give it a little bit of topspin because it is a theatrical enterprise we're talking about.

Reba: What came first, acting or martial arts?

Brandon Lee: I've always wanted to be an actor. It's the only career I've tried to pursue. I started learning martial arts with my dad right about the time I could walk, so that's always been more of a personal pursuit. I didn't ever consciously pursue the martial arts as a means of getting into show business. It's come about that I get the chance to do it in this film, and probably in films I continue to do, but it's just a skill that I have to some degree and that I get to use in this film and maybe in other films. But hopefully, a couple films from now, one film from now, I get the chance to play characters, not a martial artist, then I just won't draw on it.

Reba: When you were a kid and you moved around a lot, what kind of foundation did it give you?

Brandon Lee: Well, we moved around so much when I was a kid, and we moved from language to language and culture to culture too, not just like Oklahoma to California or something; I mean, at least it's still English and everybody's still white. I mean, we moved from Hong Kong to Los Angeles a lot when I was growing up as we were following my father's career. I didn't have too much of a problem with it. There was kind of always a certain sense of separateness just from being my father's son, in other people's eyes, so every school I'd go I'd have to find the alpha dog, you have to find the alpha dog, the guy on the playground, or he'd find you. And then you'd kick the living hell out of him, and everything would be okay.

Reba: Did they feel like they had to take you on because you had a famous father?

Brandon Lee: When I was a kid, when I was young, in the beginning of high school, I always had a problem in every new school I would go to. But it's the old "hired gun" syndrome, right?

Reba: Do you ever get scared? I mean, you look so together, but do you ever get scared?

Brandon Lee: I certainly got scared, yeah, when I was a kid, all the time. It was a drag.

Reba: Does anything scare you now?

Brandon Lee: Women, women, I don't understand women at all. So, if you ever figure it out, and you can bottle it, explain it to me, that would be great, okay?

Reba: What's the most dangerous thing you've ever done?

Brandon Lee: Well, I did this film in Hong Kong and see, Hong Kong filmmaking, it's a whole different ballgame than American filmmaking. They don't have a lot of the safety considerations that we have over here. And there was this stunt in this movie, which was called Legacy of Rage, where I was supposed to be standing next to an oil tanker that was just filled with bombs, and then I was supposed to take three big running steps—and it was on fire—and jump off this cliff, and it was a forty-foot-high fall down into some cigarette boxes with mattresses on top of them. And I was like twenty-one at the time and I thought, "This is great. It'll be fun." So, on the day, we got ready to do it, the guy had his finger on the button, and I swear to God I took like one step and the guy pushed the button too soon and this thing exploded and it was like this big, hot hand just picked me up and threw me over the cliff, and my pants caught on fire. And so I fell about forty feet and hit—I just hit the edge of the pad—and then bounced once and hit the ground. And I was okay, and my pants went out when they hit the pad, and we got it on film. It was great.

Reba: Why would you go back and do more?

Brandon Lee: It's fun. I mean, to certain extent, it's playing games; you get the chance to do things that, when you were kids, that's how you did things, right? You set up situations then you pretended you're in them and it's fun.

Reba: What drives you?

Brandon Lee: Well, it's always really great to do something that you haven't done before, and it's always really great to do something that you didn't think you can do. And I think that the feeling that you get when you do that, namely something when you trod on the ground you have yet to step on, the feeling that you get when you need to do it to get it.

Reba: When you walk onto this film set the first time, did you get butterflies knowing that you're responsible for the choreographing of the martial arts scenes?

Brandon Lee: Yeah. *Rapid Fire* was the first film that I starred in America, and it was the first film that I'm getting credit for doing the choreography on. And all the way through the entire production I felt like somebody from 20th Century Fox in some suit was going to walk onto the set and they could either have said "this is the worst film that anyone has ever made and we're going to shut down production" or they could have said "this is the best film we've ever seen, here's a million dollars," and I would have been equally nonplussed either way because that's how I was. I just had no idea what was going on. I just show up every day and try to do the best job I could and then go home every day and go, "Oh, God, I'm never going to work again."

Reba: Can you speak Chinese?

Brandon Lee: I speak Cantonese. My accent is not so great anymore and my vocabulary is not so great anymore, but I do speak it, and I speak it in the film. I spoke it as a kid. I mean, I grew up there, so yes.

Reba: Let's get to love scenes. Were you comfortable doing them?

Brandon Lee: The entire process is kind of a forced reality. We get into a room and then we pretend that a lot of it isn't there and we pretend that a lot of things that aren't there are, and it's never more intensified than when you're doing a love scene, this most personal thing between two people. I mean, there's the lights and there's the grips and there's the camera and there's the director telling us, "Okay, now do this. Now do that," but it helped make things less uncomfortable because, you know, everybody has a deep-seated neurosis about that sort of thing.

Reba: Is acting what you thought it was going to be?

Brandon Lee: Yeah, it is. I grew up around the business—although strangely enough, after my father passed away, we really weren't around the business anymore because we didn't continue to have a lot of contact with people in the business, so I had a pretty suburban regular childhood, and then just kind of got back into the business as I got a little bit older and could do things on my own.

Reba: Did your mother mind that you were going to be an actor?

Brandon Lee: My mother, especially when I was younger, when

I was first starting out when I was eighteen, nineteen, twenty—it's not that she minded, it's just that she went through one of the hardest experiences you can go through in this business, which is all of the furor and flak that surrounded my father's career after he passed away. And how people are, how journalists are, and how the press is, and how the marketing machine is. I mean, they'll do anything to make a buck. So anyway, my mother lived through a lot of that with my father and with her family trying to deal with that, and she was at the time in her mid-twenties. So, I think she never tried to stop me from acting or dissuade me, she just wanted me to be really aware of what can happen. And the thing is, I always think to myself, no matter what happens to me in my career, it's probably never going to get as weird as it already was. It was already really weird; it's probably not going to get any weirder.

Reba: We're getting to the end, I mean, and thank you for all the good words, but who are your heroes growing up?

Brandon Lee: My heroes growing up. Well, Robert M. Pirsig was one of my big heroes, the guy who wrote Zen and the Art of Motorcycle Maintenance. Hunter S. Thompson, another one of my big heroes. Hunter, if you're out there, I really want to meet you sometime, go hang at your place in Colorado. I don't know, Jack Kerouac. I love Jack Kerouac and Neal Cassady, those guys. Krishnamurti. Actors who's around now? I mean, you can always say De Niro and Hoffman and Pacino and Nicholson and those guys, but that's just a given, and Brando, of course. But I like Tom Hanks a lot. I mean, nobody ever told me I looked like him, but I do like him.

Reba: It's funny, in your list of heroes, you didn't mention any action films.

Brandon Lee: Well, my father. As a man now, getting to look at another man's work, like trying to say, "Okay, he's not my father, I'm just looking at his work as objectively as possible," I admired him tremendously. My father was a great man, and he did so much more and would have done so much more than most people probably are aware of who have just seen him in films. I mean, he had a degree in philosophy from an American university. He wrote books and screenplays, and I'm sure he would have branched out of the action genre and done so many tremendous things had he had the time.

Reba: Do you find that you were treated differently because you're Bruce Lee's son, and maybe they make it harder for you because you are?

Brandon Lee: Oh, that's a strange question. I certainly deal with being my father's son when I deal with other people's opinions or expectations of me. But I can't really blame people for that. If you didn't know someone, you had never met them, you weren't familiar with their work because, you know, let's face it: at this point my career I don't have a wide body of work for people to be familiar with, therefore it doesn't strike me as particularly strange that their first expectation or opinion of me would be based upon what they do know, which is that I'm Bruce Lee's son. But it's not a particular hardship or anything. In fact, I think it's something that's an asset.

Reba: When you sat in an audience and saw their reaction, what did you feel?

Brandon Lee: Yeah, that was the first time I had seen the film with an audience, and it was a learning experience in other ways too. I've seen the film, and I don't know if I would do this again, but this is the first time I've really been through this particular wringer, so I decided to go through it full boat. I've seen it a couple different times with a couple different audiences, and each time it's been a learning experience. You'll see some moment and you thought, "God, this is a great moment. We're going to kill them with this moment" and it just doesn't work, it falls flat on its face, you know, and you learn something from it. Or you'll see a moment that you just thought was a throwaway, it was just going to go away and it really gets people and you say, "Wow, okay," and you learned something from that. But in the end, I mean, you have to do the work from what you have to offer, what you feel strongly about. It can be very dangerous to start making choices in your acting career or in your work particularly based on what you think an audience's expectations are going to be.

Rapid Fire was only Brandon Lee's second major studio film. He was filled with life and energy as I watched him box and do karate, and cross training. I must admit, I got tired just watching all this activity. After the interview was over, I watched as my film crew shot him doing publicity stills for the film, and it was a very sexy shoot.

Once I had finished shooting all the video publicity materials, Brandon Lee went to Wilmington, North Carolina, where he died on the set of *The Crow* because of a prop gun and a fake bullet in March 1993.

17
ROBIN WILLIAMS

After struggling to get a usable interview out of a young Macaulay Culkin for Home Alone 2, I thought I could tackle anyone on any subject. Silly me. I had never interviewed Robin Williams. My first encounter with Williams was in December 1992 for the film Toys. I did a lot of research for this interview, but it didn't prepare me for what it would be like to have to sit down and have a conversation with Robin Williams. It was difficult to get straight answers to my questions because he wanted to do a comedy routine on every one of them. At first, I was thrilled to have my own comedy show and then realized this comedy wall was Robin's way of not letting me know what made him tick. It was a clever way to hide his feelings. What I did like about him was his willingness to answer the questions, even though he did it his way.

Reba: Where does the humor come from? Do you think you're born funny?

Robin Williams: If you get dropped. That's what happened to me. I was in a drug store with this lovely lady named Susie was taking care of me and I fell off the chair and I think everything changed from that moment.

Reba: When you were young, were you aware that you were funny or were you just different?

Robin Williams: Well, I knew when Mom took me to the zoo and the monkeys came to the edge of the cage and went, "One of ours."

No. Was I aware that I was different? Even then I wasn't aware. I wasn't that different when I was young. Oh, the little free-eyed boy. Why don't we bring bowling ball out to play? No, I don't know. I wasn't that different as a child where people went, "Oh, will you play with me?"

Reba: Where does it come from?

Robin Williams: It come from a cesspool of consciousness. It comes from the shallow end of the gene pool. It comes from wanting just to play and mess with things and have a good time most of the time. This is much cheaper than therapy. It's very freeing, you know, because you can talk about things, the good and the bad and get it out as another person on stage, especially. I think comedy is the thing if you free yourself up something happens, and you find wonderful stuff.

Reba: Was it difficult to go home and tell your father about going into show business?

Robin Williams: Well, he said that. He said, "Listen, if you really love it, I support you on that," which was great. And he said, "But I want you to have an alternate profession just in case you can't find work." He recommended welding, either that or animal proctology. Prepare yourself for the wild kingdom. You know, it's very difficult to have your hand up in elephant's ass going, "And how are we today, Samba?" You have a guidance counselor in school that basically recommended things for you that you know that says, "We've actually done your personality profile and then we do believe in animal proctology. That's the only place you should go, or comedy. Your choice. Either way, you're dealing with assholes." So, it's like you're trying to…you play with it and see what you can do, and that's why Dad was great, he said that I…he was wonderful that way because somehow, I think he saw that I really wanted to do it, and that's great.

Reba: When did you know you wanted to do it?

Robin Williams: It didn't really happen until college, and I went to the improv group and it was a blast, and all of a sudden I found a place where I could use everything that I knew and have fun with it.

Reba: Does everybody expect you to always be on? Give me a straight answer.

Robin Williams: To always be on. No, I can play dead, and I can come back. And they do sometimes expect it, but not always. I mean, but most of the time I enjoy being on because it's allowing me to use my mind. For me, everything out there was something to play off of.

Reba: I thought the best of all the research was that if you keep me laughing, I'll never find out who you are.

Robin Williams: Ooh, that's lovely.

I felt prepared when I sat down with him again for the *Mrs. Doubtfire* interview. I thought that I was ready for anything he was going to throw at me.

Reba: *Mrs. Doubtfire* gave you the chance to wear a mask where you got to hear things.

Robin Williams: Oh, it was great, yes, sometimes we'd be shooting in public places and in the early days I could sneak off and just listen as people were talking about, "Who's in the movie?" "It's Robin Williams." They'd ask me, like, "Where is he?" "I don't know, Dear, he is so strange, I don't know. They have to strap him down." And you could just sit down and listen to people talk to you about even the movie or be like literally this other person. Someone tried to help me across the street, "I'm fine." and "Put your penis away." You know, it's like, "Don't do that." But they treat you in a whole different way, which is great. I walked into shops, strange shops, and it was fun because they had not a clue it was me.

Reba: Can I ask one more personal thing about you?

Robin Williams: Please throw it out. Throw it in there.

Reba: When your marriage went under and you wanted to make sure that the relationship with your son stayed solid, did you use humor?

Robin Williams: No, it's actually the opposite, I just used time. It was a basic thing, just spending time is very precious and quality time and going from just Nintendo time, which is not as much as they may call it interactive, it's not that. Playing, contacting, getting to know him, sharing with him, sharing my past with him so he knows who I am and I know who he is, and then we have a bond. And bonding just doesn't happen, just because "you are my kid, we're bonding." Yeah, there's a certain genetic bonding there, but then there's other things that have to be nurtured. It's a tie that has to be taken care of and it needs time and energy and effort and concentration and listening and playing and being there for him, being an adult, but being that kid sometimes too. It's all these things that make you closer, and you have to work at it, it doesn't just happen. It doesn't just go like, "I'm your dad, you know me." No, it's there and you have that love, don't give up on it. That's really important stuff.

Reba: Your mother gave you your comic instincts.

Robin Williams: Well, I think I developed them so I could make contact with her. She was funny, and I found one way of, "Hey, mom, notice me," was to be funny. And, you know, she was, "Oh, you're funny," and that way we kind of bonded. That was our bonding comedy.

Reba: You were voted funniest in school, so obviously you were funny at a young age?

Robin Williams: Only in the senior year of high school did it kind of started to appear, and then freshman year of college it was even more. I found an improv group and I loved the improv group so much and I never went to my economics classes and failed all those, but I loved the Improv group and it turned out to be the thing that I kept doing for years and the basis for what I still do.

Reba: Okay. You have the power to erupt volcanically when you're performing. It's not where did that come from, it's how come you're not afraid what people are going to think of you?

Robin Williams: The truth is at the time, I don't remember, it's afterward, "What did I say? Do you think that was offensive? Do you think people be angry?" I mean, because at the time you don't have any control over it. It kind of comes out of you. It is kind of like being possessed, especially when some of the riffs just, you don't know where they're going. So today I got to do a couple of my own with a little fire. You could feel it happening and then you don't know what's going to happen to the very end. And once it's over with, then you start worrying about the consequences. "Did I really say…oh, really? Oh, no. Oh, no." "Oh, did I go too far?" Because then you realize only after it's over what you'd actually done. "Did I really take out my penis and make it a puppet? Did I actually call him like the little weasel? Make the weasel dance? Did I do that?" "Yes, you did." "And what else did I do?" "Well, notice how hairy I am." "Okay. That's it. Is that all?" "Yep." Okay. You see, those are the things that when afterward, I will go, "Oh, no," but now I'm actually getting to the point where I just say it's beyond politically correct. It's like it's only personally correct. If you believe in it, you got to stand by it and there will be people who will be pissed off.

Reba: And are you comfortable now stepping back, relaxing and knowing when to stop and just slow down…?

Robin Williams: Yes, it took a while. It took taking a vacation after finishing *Doubtfire*. I went to Italy, and I finally relaxed. It was literally because I didn't know what day it was, I'm like, "Is it Tuesday? It's Friday. Wow," because it was just being in Italy, a very timeless place. You know, you're wandering around through these walled cities and here is a walled city named Luca, which is incredible. But it is for me, I finally learned to say no, to stop, "Robbie, enjoy life. Have a best time." And then you see you have beautiful children, beautiful wife. You have a house, and you have a mind. Okay, Robbie, enjoy it.

Why you wandering around all this time looking for the golden boy? Well, it comes every year. The golden boy has no genitals and big clue. Why they called him Oscar? It's a nice thing, but Robbie, you have a life, hold up the baby. There's your Academy Award. Thank you for another good one.

I started a ritual with Williams after my *Toys* interview and continued it for the next five interviews: I always went to the bathroom in his suite before I sat down with him because all he wanted to do was make me laugh, which would ruin the audio track. I controlled my laughter, because my bladder was empty, which was why I made a big deal of the bathroom gig. He was a maniac hilarious life of the party type guy, though I now understood he used his quick humor to mask his feelings of depression. Once again, I was looking to find the real Robin Williams and very little of it did come through. I always felt that I had the upper hand when conducting interviews, but Robin Williams made me aware I still had a lot to learn.

His death came as a surprise to all. I didn't know that Robin had been suffering from Parkinson's disease and dementia, which made him depressed and filled with anxiety and paranoia. I realized he felt he had no place else to go. His death became global news. His daughter, Zelda Williams, put out a statement: "The world is a little darker, less colorful, and less filled with laughter in his absence." I will miss him forever and will never forget the time we spent together.

18
SEAN CONNERY

When the invitation came for a Sean Connery interview, I was in heaven because I loved James Bond. In doing the research for the interview, I found out that Connery was born in 1930 and had won not only an Academy Award but also three Golden Globes—not bad for a man who started out as a milkman, then became a model, a bodybuilder, and eventually an actor. He was the first actor to portray the character of James Bond, starring in seven Bond films. I couldn't wait to ask him about Bond as his was my favorite iteration. Connery gave me butterflies just looking at him during the interview.

I had an uphill battle for this interview because his personal publicist did not like me; she even tried to get me fired. She made it very clear to me, in fact poking her finger in my face, that I was not to ask him any questions about James Bond. I knew that she had enough power to destroy my career, so I was very careful. She sat next to Connery while I did the interview, a first for me as I had been doing these junket interviews for two years and never had a publicist sit in the room. Usually, they watched from the control room.

Reba: It's very interesting looking back on your career. It seems that a lot of your characters share the same traits. If you can't remember them, I made a list. I'll give you a few of them and you tell me what this feels like: brains, cunning, intensity, leadership, a set of ethics, individualistic, and wit. Intentional? These kinds of men you've played, you bring to the screen?

Sean Connery: Well, I'd like to think they are all attributes of mine, but maybe it's the characters I choose to display it.

Reba: What determines a project before you commit to it?

Sean Connery: Well, for myself, it's invariably the writing in retrospect I think it something that would appeal to me, get my attention, and think, Wow, I'd like to see this and then I get the enthusiasm for it and then I say I want to do it. I don't think too much through in terms of what the location will be like or what the hardships will be like or the difficulties one will encounter, and in a funny way, I never seem to learn that.

Reba: Well, if The Man Who Would Be King is any indication, I heard that you wanted to dance with Michael's driver because he was better looking. Is that true?

Sean Connery: That's absolutely true. We were in Morocco in some wonderful places, one of the places was called Tiffletoot or some thing, and the hotel number was one—gives you an idea of how many people are there. And I went to the wash basin and turned the tap and had brown dust.

I had a big wagon, which I used as my dressing room, my office, and everything, and I had everything I owned from the film was in that Volkswagen bus. And I'm driving back to the hotel, I'd taken off my turban and my face was black, and I was wearing a caftan, it was very hot. There was some riots in the bushes with something going wrong somewhere, and I drove straight into the military guys who'd fired the guns and everything. I didn't speak any French or Moroccan and these guys were serious dragging me out of the car and purely by luck one of them recognized me as James Bond. Otherwise, I'd have still been there.

Reba: Do you feel like you've had, like, two careers? James Bond and now this wonderful career—not that James Bond wasn't a wonderful career, don't get me wrong, but this is a wonderful career.

Sean Connery: Well, yes, mind you the proportion of actual successful movies is probably sixty-forty, but then it depends what you determine is commercial.

Reba: What makes you happy? Aren't you happy playing all these interesting men? Not that Bond wasn't.

Sean Connery: Why are you so defensive about Bond?

Reba: I heard I had to be real careful and not ask you about Bond.

Sean Connery: Really? What do you think I would do?

Reba: I hope kiss me, but I don't think that's the way it works in interviews. [Rolls his head back laughing.] But I remember having my heart pound when you said, "Bond. James Bond," and I thought you did it just for me!

Sean Connery: But, of course, I did!

Reba: Can I go back to your childhood? When you grew up, did you know you were poor? And did it matter?

Sean Connery: Did I know I was poor? Of course, you know you're poor. What you don't know is when you're really very young and you only have your one set of values, which is in the area where you are, and everything really related directly to economics. I mean, there was never any discussion in the house of, "Oh, I think I'm going to go on a holiday this year." Holidays was when the school closed, and you'd just have to get out of the house and come back when it was getting dark so that the whole lifestyle was in a tenement building so it was not conducive to considerations. What you were aware of when you delivered milk like I did was when you went to these houses when you were nine, and then you saw a whole different lifestyle and it was brought home to you, when the war came and you're not allowed to go to school because they might bomb the schools with them teaching in the houses and it was okay to bring the milk to the house but they wouldn't want you in the house to teach you.

Reba: Looking back on this career of thirty-plus years, are you surprised and comfortable with fame?

Sean Connery: Sometimes more than not. It's different if you're dealing with something like we're talking about the film. This thing, you're a part of it, I'm a part of it, the camera crew is a part, and I'm understand it's the mechanics of doing what one does. The elements of outside when it's a bit more extraneous, then it's different. Then it's much more improvised.

Reba: But you look at me and my heart pounds and I get goosebumps, so I mean, that's what fame is to me.

Sean Connery: [Laughs]

Reba: Thank you, that's what it is!

His publicist knew I had avoided Bond and yet my one retort had set her off. I had never met this woman before the junket and had no idea why she had a problem with me.

When Sean Connery's film *The Rock* came out, his publicist, Nancy, told the studio Connery did not want to be interviewed by me, which was not true as he did not even know who I was. It did not matter to the studio, and they still wanted me to create my video profiles for the film. The studio got someone else to ask the Connery questions and I did the rest. Best of all, I got paid for all the profiles no matter who asked the questions. I produced all five video publicity interviews for *The Rock* and they got huge airplay.

I owe most of my career to gay men and three women who gave me a chance. I made them look good because results don't lie, just people. That's what it was like in Hollywood—women not supporting each other. But just like in the movies, this story had a happy ending. Nancy lost most of her big stars, and I got to interview all of them.

19
SANDRA BULLOCK

I always enjoyed interviewing Sandra Bullock. She delivered a terrific performance and gave me a great interview in *When the Party's Over*—a big role in a small film that no one saw. The two television series she did never got renewed, and yet she kept working but never grabbed the brass ring. I knew that *Speed* was going to be her winning role and she was going to be a star, so I concentrated on giving the world a candid profile of this soon-to-be-in-demand actress.

Reba: I get the feeling you really like what you're doing.

Sandra Bullock: Nine times out of ten, I mean, you have the days where you wish you just not gotten out of bed. But for the most part, yeah, I like what I'm doing. But also, when I go in, and I meet with the people who might be doing a project, if I don't like them, I'm not going to do it. Because it's going to make me bad if I feel that there's a bad vibe and they don't have a really good sense of humor, there's no point in me taking things further because if I don't have a really fun place to work in, then I don't do a good job. So pretty much I test out the waters first to make sure.

Reba: Aren't you afraid that if you do that you won't work again?

Sandra Bullock: You know what, every actor after their job is like, "Maybe I'll never work again," but I have other skills, like I can do construction work, I can waitress, and now I can be a bus driver, because I just got my license. So, if you're insecure, as a lot of actors tend to be because it's a very harsh business, you're always going to think you're never going to work again. But it's your career.

It's your life and if you don't do what you want to do, you're going to be eighty years old going, I wish I had not felt forced to take things where I was going to be unhappy rather than just go with what's going to make me happy and hope that'll lead to something else that'll make me happy. So, I've been really lucky so far. I've had a couple of bad experiences but that was at the beginning of when I didn't know any better; now I know better, so I'm wise.

Reba: Are you superstitious?

Sandra Bullock: I'm superstitious in the sense that I believe what goes around comes around always, always, always, always. So every time I do something really bad, and I'm conscious of what I'm doing, at least I can stop myself before I do it. You know, I'll get halfway through what I was getting ready to do because I know that eventually I'll be having a really good time. So, in that respect, I'm really superstitious, not like in black cats or railroad tracks. Things like that don't bother me, but in the sense that what goes around comes around, I adhere to that.

Reba: One of the things I love about you—and I don't want to embarrass you...

Sandra Bullock: But you're going to.

Reba: I'm going to anyway. It's your sense of timing. Do you have a clock in you? You deliver lines with such timing, that they're just ordinary lines, and then all of a sudden, they come out of Sandra's mouth.

Sandra Bullock: Stupid.

Reba: No, they come out funny. It's not that you're just outrageously funny, but your warmth comes through with comic timing?

Sandra Bullock: My father has an incredible sense of humor. So as a child, everything was about great story, telling great jokes. Everything was funny in our household. I mean, anytime at the dinner table, you could, you know, fling something across the table or embarrass somebody or bring up a topic that's unacceptable for the dinner table. It was done. So, I mean, that's the atmosphere. And it's a surprise to you I didn't get a lot of etiquette in my upbringing, but I didn't. So, I think in the way that I've learned to deal with life to make it a lot less painful a lot of times, I just joke about everything. So, I think if you just do it enough. And the funniest things in life come out of real situations. You know, I'll fall down a set of stairs, yes, I broke my leg. But it was awfully funny as I was coming down thirty-six flights, and if somebody at the bottom is laughing, I understand that because my first instinct would be to laugh then call 911. So that's the way I look at things is, yes, they might be incredibly tragic at that time, but you can't control your reactions to it, so I just blurt things out and as long as they're honest then if the line is written well and a funny line and you say it honestly, it's always going to come out funny. And the writers wrote funny lines. You just have to make them work in whatever way you can because sometimes you can say it be written brilliantly and it comes out of your mouth like pebbles, so you just have to kind of work it. Usually going back to the truthful real way totally straight is what makes it work.

Reba: Your love scenes are getting more and more interesting.

Sandra Bullock: You know what, they're not. Have you noticed that I haven't had any real love scene? Where's that love scene you touch? The person thinks I'm like in shards of glass kissing somebody. I read the scripts and, like, what happened to a Sea of Love, Ellen Barkin opportunity? I don't get those. I know I should take offense.

Reba: I think after this one, you're going to get it because that, that kissing scene—

Sandra Bullock: Well, I was obviously kissing him. I mean, our lips were touching. You know, that's what I liked about it, too, because when I first saw it in the looping stage, I was incredibly embarrassed.

Because I know there was something very sweet about it. And when you're there, you don't see it because you're worrying about where your elbows are going to landing at the time. And you're like, "How long are we supposed to kiss until somebody says stop kissing?" Or if you keep going, you think they're gonna say, "Cut. Cut. That was way too long." So, you never know what the boundaries are so you always keep it relatively technical. But when you genuinely like somebody you work with, you just like them as a person, I think that is always going to show through. I don't know if he genuinely likes me, but I think he's a really sweet person. So, I think if you like somebody it's going to show through. You can't stand them. Then I think look on your face be something more like you're kissing them rather than a smile.

Reba: Do you remember the old days when you wanted to be an actress? Or is it so far away now?

Sandra Bullock: I remember what I was raised with, which was my mother being an opera singer in Germany at the time. The greatest babysitting service for her was just to shove me in the operas with her. In every opera, there's a role of like a poor scraggly kid. I was the poor scraggly kid. And so that's the way I started. I have a sister, younger sister, and we were definitely made up of two separate piles of genes. I was the common-sense practical joker who was very physical, and she was, she's incredibly logical, and book smart and brilliant that way. So that's why she's becoming a lawyer. I became the actor. So, with my parents, being artists, I think I just knew nothing else. You know, there wasn't anything else that I had a desire to passionately do except for dance. And then that I wasn't passionate enough not to eat the junk food or to go to nine hours of training to sort of go to that duration of torture in order to be brilliant at what I did. I don't mind failing. I have no problem being criticized and failing in what I do in my profession now because I have such a good time. You know, I chose it, I made my bed. So, you know, people are going to be hard on you. But I've got until ninety to perfect it. And so, if I should live to ninety, hopefully, I will have ninety-eight percent of it right.

Reba: Is it what you thought it was going to be? Is it that magic?

Sandra Bullock: Yeah, it's exactly what I thought it would be. Only because at the very beginning, I had a tough, couple tough times, where I learned early on what not to put myself into, what situations to avoid. So, like I was saying, you meet nice people, and you meet people that you click with. So, I've been fortunate enough to click with some pretty great people and been given parts and films that were a lot of fun and great. So, yes, it's everything that I thought it was along with all the hardships and all the pain that goes along with it. But, you know, I kind of welcome the hardships and the pain because once you get that, it makes you just work all that much harder.

Reba: I'm wondering, does anything scare you?

Sandra Bullock: It should. What frightens me is that since I started, I have no problem. It's two different way, like in my work, I have no problem barreling into things, I can just put on blinders and whatever the mess I make, I'll deal with it later, which is good for what I do. In my private life, on the other hand, I've set up so many boundaries for myself, like with people I won't overstep boundaries. So, it's like, I have two completely different sides to me. So, what frightens me more is what I do in my work I can't always bring over into my private life. And I'd love to be able to be more courageous in my private life like I am in my work. So that frightens me that I can't make the two meet. But then again, it might be a good thing that the two are on two totally different planes to keep me sort of levelheaded, maybe.

Reba: What about fame? Is it what you thought it was going to be?

Sandra Bullock: I'm not in a category that, you know, you have Keanu in or Julia Roberts or Sylvester Stallone. I'm not even there and I honestly don't think I'll ever get there because some people are just cut out for it. Some people, when they walk into a room, you go, "Oh, my God, they have something," you just can't help but watch them. Other people just kind of walk into a room, plop down on the couch, and start eating at the buffet. I'm the buffet eater. You know, I don't think I have the desire or that whatever it is that people have to be the superstar.

Reba: But you have a drive. I mean, let's not underestimate the roles you've been doing, they're all different.

Sandra Bullock: Yeah, I made a point to do. I mean, every time I finished one, I'll take my time finding something completely different because I get so bored with that side of myself. You don't want to do it again. So I've been very lucky and very cautious and had to fight tooth and nail because people, like, "She's not a Southern belle, don't bring her to me." But then someone will say, "I think she can do it." I've met great people who've taken a chance in placing me in things or trusted my craft enough. But there are hundreds of thousands of actors and artists out there who have drive who never make it to another level or make it to whatever level they aspire to make it to, and they're brilliant—there's so many great actors out there. You go to theater down in a hole in a closet somewhere. And you can see actors that will just blow your mind. And you know, that has drive, those people have drive. For some reason, some people seem to make it to the next level. I don't know what it is. I don't know why I've been fortunate enough to be where I am. But you know, don't question it. Don't fix it. If it ain't broke.

Reba: Have you ever been at the wrong place at the wrong time?
Sandra Bullock: Yeah, you don't hear about all the times I was in the wrong place falling on my face. People don't want to hear about the wrong place at the wrong time. I think because I've been in a lot of wrong places at the wrong time is made me that much more determined to find the right place. And every wrong place will teach you where not to go next time. So, you know, I've fallen on my face so many times. I've been, you know, I've had my share of stuff. But without that I wouldn't be where I was sitting. So, you know, I'm not going to complain. Of course, I'll go home and, every once in a while, complain about it, but if it wasn't for one thing, it wouldn't be for another. So, I try to keep relatively optimistic.

The story behind the film *Hope Floats* was an interesting one. The only way *Speed 2* could be made was if she agreed to star in it. Bullock did it for 20th Century Fox and the studio returned the favor by funding her passion project, which she starred in and produced. Both films made the studio money, but more importantly, it gave a big bump to Bullock and her production company. When I interviewed her again for *Hope Floats* I found this Q&A moment.

Reba: I was one of those outcasts, surprised to hear you were, too.

Sandra Bullock: Absolutely. I spent most of my life being the outcast until I figured out the brass ring was this click. And unfortunately, I, being a gymnast and a drama geek, I said, "Well, I can be a cheerleader. I can flip and do these things." And the day that I became the cheerleader, which was a freak in itself that I got in and still nobody understands, was the day that it was like the heaven's gates opened in terms of the acceptance factor. And by the end of my second year, I was like, "What have I done?" Because I was like, one of those people that people constantly were beating up on or teasing. And I was so glad for that. Because once I left, I know my children will be kind. Kids can be pretty, pretty cruel. So, it just, it makes you a better person. I think being the outcast makes you a humble, kind person, I really do.

Reba: I think you deal with failure easier.

Sandra Bullock: Oh, God, if you expect it, then it's hard for somebody who's always succeeded and had the brass ring because you're not prepared for real life, when nine times out of ten, you're not going to get that. So, the education factor is, the learning curve is far greater when you've been kicked around a little bit.

As a freelance interviewer, I never knew when I would get another job or whom would I work with, so it really thrilled me when Teri Ritzer Meyer became the Vice President of Publicity at Buena Vista International, the releasing arm for all Disney films in 1995. The first job she gave me was for the film called While You Were Sleeping starring Sandra Bullock.

20
HARRISON FORD, AGAIN

When I was invited twenty years later to do an interview with Harrison Ford for *Air Force One*, I was curious about how it would go. The last time I had interviewed him he was still an up-and-coming actor and now he was a superstar. I knew that he didn't suffer fools lightly and had no trouble putting you in your place and even cutting off the interview. I knew Ford did not know who I was except that I worked for Buena Vista International and was doing the generic interview for the world. When I walked into his suite and said, "Hello, don't worry about the questions as I know all the answers," it must have struck a chord as he relaxed and smiled.

Reba: You play larger than life heroes on film, are you getting back at the bullies that beat you up at school?

Harrison Ford: What happened was I moved to a new school and I was about twelve years old and there was already a well-formed society in that school, and because I was the outsider and didn't fit in, I became the school sport of throwing me off of the edge of the parking lot down a twenty-foot bank every recess. And I don't really remember how it started, but I remember my reaction was just to pick up myself, dust myself off, and crawl up to the top again. I struggled and tried to get away but my theory in those days was that if you hit somebody back it was going to make them even madder and then you'd end up getting hurt worse. I never really fought back. One of the attendant factors was I developed great sympathy from the girls, so while I was getting thrown off the edge of the hill at recess, I was gaining benefits that last through the rest of the day. I only told this story years later in response to a very specific question, and the press has been intrigued by it.

Reba: In the beginning you had terrible stage fright; why did you continue?

Harrison Ford: I was a bit offended by my failure to be able to overcome this fear that surged through my body. I'd never met that challenge before in my life. I'd never been so afraid of something, and it challenged me to overcome it. I had not gone easily into being on stage. I had taken a film course in drama without realizing that it involved a stage appearance. So, I found myself for the very first time on stage, and it was nerve-racking. My first ambition was to overcome that fear. Then I became involved, after that fear dissipated, in the other processes that made acting interesting to me. I finally came to develop enough interests in those processes to make a lifetime of it. What came along after the fear were two things: the interest in storytelling and the effect that was created between myself and the audience. When I'm engaged in storytelling, I'm much more specifically interested in how to tell this story that we're telling on screen. In the process of telling stories that were essentially about our common humanity it began to help me find a place in society that I hadn't felt before.

Reba: Did you teach yourself to be a carpenter?

Harrison Ford: I think one either has a certain manual dexterity or not, and I have a little manual dexterity. And then I acquired the tool skills to work with the tools, not against them, and then I had a basic understanding of how the whole business worked and a respect for it. I think that all together it helped me to learn carpentry easily. It was something I wanted to learn. The same with acting: it was something I wanted to learn. It was a little more difficult to acquire the skills of acting than carpentry because nobody wanted to pay me to learn on the job. During that short period of time when I studied acting, the way it was taught to me was different to the way that I finally came to understand how to work it for myself and the people that I worked with.

Reba: Were you hard on yourself?

Harrison Ford: I've always been a useful critic of myself. I don't take any great pleasure in watching myself after the fact when it's all said and done, but I do enjoy watching the work as it develops in order that I might do it better. I'm quite happy to run back to the video monitor and see the take so that I can know that if I stand two steps over it's going to be a better, stronger shot. So, I know how to self-correct as much as possible. And I'm very interested in doing the best job that I can, given the extensive circumstances of filmmaking, which is you have a limited amount of time and money to spend in any given moment. I think it's very useful to be able to look at yourself and make helpful self-corrections.

Reba: Do you use a stunt guy for action scenes?

Harrison Ford: No, it's like a dance routine. You choreograph them and then there's storytelling and choices in the storytelling involved in how you choreograph a physical scene. There is discipline involved in controlling your emotions and your body so that nobody gets hurt, and you don't get hurt. There is not really adrenaline involved unless it's leaping across a chasm or something like that. It's a skill that you develop over time and through experience, and I enjoy it. I have a good time with the guys running, jumping, and falling and rolling around on the floor and working up a sweat.

Reba: Are you going to tell me when you get slapped it doesn't hurt you, how comes it hurts me? [He laughed, the only time he ever laughed in an interview with me.]

Harrison Ford: Well, you've got to stop going where people slap you. I get paid enough money to stand there all day long and get slapped. If you're getting slaps for free, you're going to the wrong place. But I'm making a living standing there getting slapped, so it doesn't hurt me, no. And Gary is the slapper in this case, and Gary has enough stagecraft to know how to use his hands, to loosen limp and to slap me in the right way.

Reba: I'm sure you know you're famous. How do you deal with it?

Harrison Ford: The problem that I have is that the most valuable thing to give up in your life is anonymity, is to be able to pass unnoticed through life when you want to. For an actor, the most valuable thing is to be able to observe human nature unencumbered by your presence. Those are big things to give up. I have learned over a period of time as I have become more and more in public view to deal with the reality in that situation. There are practical means for staying as small as you can in public and not attracting attention to yourself. It's very useful to me in selling movies to be well-known.

When I do an interview, I only concentrate on what the star is saying so that I can come back with a follow-up question if I need to. I was really surprised when Ford looked at me—which was really my cameraman behind me—and said, "put another tape in, we are not finished." I never heard the camera go off, he did. What surprisedme most was his reaction to this interview; he could have graciously said thank you very much, nice seeing you, but instead he gave me another ten minutes. Here it is.

Reba: I forgot what the question was.

Harrison Ford: We were talking, would it be impossible to have the opportunities that I have without the success that's attended some of my films, and that's what makes you "famous," if you will.

Reba: I guess it's really easy to say that you feel lucky about the things that have happened.

Harrison Ford: Real easy. In fact, it's easiest to say because it is the truth. It's easy to describe yourself as lucky when you manifestly have been lucky to be involved in the things that I've been involved in.

Reba: Do you have fun making movies?

Harrison Ford: No, I love making movies. I love the opportunity to live different lives, to work with different people on different kinds of subjects. I love getting to travel. I love playing with the big toys that are involved in movie making. I have, I think, the best job in the world.

Reba: Are there some movies that you've had more fun on than others?

Harrison Ford: Certainly, there are some experiences that are more fun to go through than others. A lot of filmmaking is very, very complex. And other times, as in the case of this film, which we call "Air Force Fun," it was a ball to go to work every day. But even when it was most difficult, it's still better than a real job, and it's demanding and rewarding and very, very engaging. That's what I look for.

Reba: Was the Indiana Jones movie difficult for you because of your age?

Harrison Ford: Well, I was thirty-five when I first did *Star Wars*, so, I was even older than that when I did *Indiana Jones*. And even in those fantasy adventure films, I found that I have the same job to do as I have to do in a straight drama like *Devil's Own* or in a film like *Air Force One*. The job is always the same, that's to help tell the story through character behavior.

Reba: Do you ever get scared?

Harrison Ford: I have trepidation occasionally about certain things. I have not, in a long time, known "abject fear," just because nobody has caused that to happen. Fear is something in my experience that only comes [snaps fingers] like that when you're unprepared for it. Most of the situations I find myself in are of my own invention. I put myself in a situation where I have to work myself out or something. Sometimes I have trepidation, sometimes I'm unsure of myself, sometimes I get in over my head, but I haven't suffered from real panic for a long, long time.

Reba: Why did you walk away from your TV career?

Harrison Ford: I never really did do well in television. I survived from small part to small part, but my ambition was always to do the kind of work, to play the kind of roles that didn't seem to occur very often in television, especially not episodic television. And episodic television, I should say, has come a long way since the days when I was doing *Love, American Style*. So, what I was anxious to do was to play with the big boys. I wanted to do ambitious kinds of films. I wanted to take on characters that were a bit more complicated and interesting to play than the kind of roles that I was playing in television. And I was aware of the fact that if I was to stay at the same place doing episodic television over and over again, I would wear out my face and never get a chance to do the kind of work that I wanted to do, which seemed only to happen in movies. And because I discovered another way of putting food on the table for my young family by doing carpentry, I was able to wait it out. Because I always knew one thing, which was that tenacity was more important than almost anything else.

I arrived in Hollywood on the metaphoric bus with a group of young people who all had a similar ambition in mind. And as the years went by, the attrition rate eliminated many of those people from the competition pool. And finally, there was only a few of us left from that entering class. And I always saw life that way, that you really had to stick it out and prevail. And along the way I learned a great deal more about my craft than I knew when I first arrived.

Once I was through with the Harrison Ford interview, I was approached by Teri Ritzer Myer—now vice president of publicity for all of Disney's films—and she wanted to know what I had done to him, as he had been so nice to me and that had not happened to any other journalist that day. I believed he recognized that I cared enough about him to do research, which shows respect.

I interviewed him twice more, and I knew he remembered me, and I never forgot him. I finally had the courage to give him the tape of our 1977 *Star Wars* interview because it was one of the worst interviews of my career and I was embarrassed. I told him it was for his children so they could see how young he was. I must admit this *Air Force One* interview was the one I loved the most.

21
NICOLAS CAGE

I was always fascinated with Nicolas Cage, who never said no to a film. He was always in the news doing something that actually was more interesting than the film he was working on. When it came to Nick Cage, I had done so many films with him that I had a hard time picking which ones I wanted to share. My first film with him was in 1993 for *Deadfall*, a terrible interview for a terrible film. He did the interview in an ugly disguise like his character and answered me like his character. I got the feeling he didn't even want to do the film, which, I thought, he took just to help his brother, Christopher Coppola, who wrote and directed it. If his name sounds familiar it was because Nick Cage is a Coppola, whose uncle, Francis Ford Coppola, was the Oscar-winning director of the *Godfather* films. He changed his name because he wanted to make it on his own—though his first break came in 1983 with the film *Rumble Fish*, directed by his uncle, who used him again later in *The Cotton Club* and in *Peggy Sue Got Married*, and by then Nick Cage was fully launched.

The Nick Cage from *Deadfall* left me dreading our next encounter.

I picked him for this book because he charmed me from then on, whether I liked the film or not.

Kiss of Death gave Nick Cage not only his best reviews so far in his career but also a chance to step in and steal the show—he wasn't even the star of the film. By now I had done three interviews in three years with him and he did recognize me, which I believe made this interview his most interesting. I know that he had fun from that first question, as the look on his face—which included a big smile—let me know we were going to have some fun. It didn't hurt that I understood where he was coming from with this character.

Reba: Now, just between you and me, it's a lot more fun to play a bad boy on the screen because maybe you can't do it in real life now that you're grown up?

Nicolas Cage: Just between you and me? Hello? Actually, yes, there is some truth in that because I'm not a bad boy in that regard. I'm not like a violent guy. I do walk away from fights, and I do avoid violence situations. So, to be able to play this guy was really like extended Halloween where I could dress up as a monster and feel like all- powerful, like the Incredible Hulk or something, which is everything that I'm not, really.

Reba: Speaking about fathers, and you'll have to help me a little bit. But there seemed to be a very interesting relationship between Junior, your character, and his father. And the tough edge, I thought, covered up the little boy that really wanted his father's approval. What do you think, was Junior really wanted to impress his father as a tough guy with acts of violence?

Nicolas Cage: He was killing because he wanted his father's approval, in my opinion. He wanted the love of his father, and the better he was a killer, the better he could kill, the more love he would probably get—if you could call it love—more approval, probably more likely. But it's interesting you say big child because that's what I wanted him to be like, this giant horrible baby, which is very insightful that you would find that because I'd almost forgotten about it. But that was an important aspect of the role. Even the name Little Junior was like this, this monster baby. And so in that regard, there's something kind of sad about the character because he is a victim of his family. I mean, what kind of father raises their child to be a hitman, his own personal hitman? It's nightmarish.

Reba: It's interesting, because you were raised so differently in a wonderful family. Did you just take for granted that everybody was raised like you with all these wonderful cultural moments?

Nicolas Cage: Well, I had a unique situation with my father and I began to realize that it was different from the other kids on the block because while they were playing baseball and football, I was having seances and charging twenty-five cents, and putting on puppet shows and radio shows, and you know, both are good. So in some ways, I wish my dad had tossed the ball a little more and I could have not made the basketball hoop for the wrong team, you know, and avoid a lot of embarrassment in school. But yes, his knowledge of literature and film definitely motivated me and inspired me. I remember him taking me to see *The Magnificent Ambersons* when I was a very young teenager, about thirteen, and was very impressionable. It did motivate me, definitely.

Reba: I know that you're comfortable being a tough guy on the screen. But is it true that when you were a kid, you weren't so tough, and that kids actually beat you up in the back of the school bus?

Nicolas Cage: It's true. Well, it was because of my Twinkie. And my mother would put a Twinkie in my lunch bag and they knew I had that cream-filled sponge cake and they went for it and would steal it. And if I said give me my lunch sack back, they would beat me up. And so I remember I woke up in the morning after collecting my older brother's cowboy boots, jeans, sunglasses, and chewing gum, and left the house with my hair greased back and I was chewing gum. I had all this attitude and went on the bus and I said I was really Richard, I'm Nikki's cousin. And if you take his Twinkie again, I'm gonna beat you up, you know, and they were like, not sure. But it was in the fact that they were not sure if it was me or it wasn't me that I suddenly thought, I can do this. I can have this attitude. I can act.

Reba: What impact did James Dean's films have on you?

Nicolas Cage: Well, I think I made the decision to go into acting. I was always able to naturally access comedy as a means of survival, as a means of making friends, as a means of not seeing the dark side of things in my own childhood. When I saw those pictures, I said, "Yes, that's what I want to do," because in particular the scene where he returns the money to his father, and is denied… When he gives the money, rather, to his father as a birthday present and is shot down essentially and does not have the love that he needs, I was heartbroken. No song, no painting, no book had ever moved me that way. And that's when I said that's what I want to do.

Reba: Because you came from such a famous creative family, was it kind of expected of you to act, or do something in the arts?

Nicolas Cage: At least not in a spoken way. I mean, my father really wanted me to be a writer. And I think I somewhat broke his heart when I decided to be an actor. But I felt the pressure of having to do something just because I could look around and I wanted to achieve something. I wanted to be able to have what my cousins had. I'd go visit them and they had very beautiful boats and remote-control walkie-talkies, toys that my brother and I didn't have and I wanted and it sort of gave me a little torch under my butt to go to work to really strive so that I could, I don't know, enjoy those things.

Reba: What has acting given you? And are you surprised?

Nicolas Cage: Well, it's given me sanity. I mean, I don't know what I would have been if I wasn't an actor. I've thought about going to go away on a merchant marine boat and try to be the next Herman Melville and write books, but it's given me the ability to take my childhood or whatever's bothered me and to use acting as a catalyst to convert it into positive energy and it's really given me a life.

Nick Cage never said no to a film. From 1993 to 2004, I interviewed him ten times and always found him to be an interesting interviewee and a fascinating man, who has never disappointed me—except for *Deadfall*. Of all the actors I have sat across from, I have missed him the most.

22
ROBERT REDFORD 2ND

I was excited to see my first superstar interviewee, Robert Redford, again after fifteen years. When I did an interview for *The Horse Whisperer* in 1998, he had no idea that I had been on the set of *The Natural*, and I didn't tell him.

Reba: You must have been very physical as a kid and I wondered if you ever thought about playing a cowboy? Because you sure look like a cowboy today.

Robert Redford: I don't think I imagined playing a cowboy in a film, but I imagined playing a cowboy. I thought I'd be one. And, in a way, I am a little bit. I'm not the cowboy like the one in the film that I play, but I have enough experience out west living in Utah and raising horses and being with animals and also developing some crops there on the land. I've had experience.

Reba: Your great love was art, and I was going to ask you, how did you go from art to acting because they don't seem alike, but, in a way, they really are.

Robert Redford: I think there's connective lines to all mediums whether it's painting or writing or acting or conducting music because you're dealing with some expression of the soul's meaning. And I think it connects that way. I think most artists quite enjoy other art, for example.

Reba: Is it really true that you were a starving artist on the Left Bank? It sounds so romantic, but you lived it.

Robert Redford: Yes, it does, but also sounds phony. But it's true, I did eat, I didn't completely starve to death, but it was rough times, but I didn't see it that way, at the time. I was only nineteen years old and it was so exciting to be in France and there were rough times, there were, which didn't hit me as hard because I was young and full of energy and enthusiasm. I was learning something new every minute of every day, and I liked the adventure of it. And I thought I also should spend that part of my life like that without anything and having to develop resources to live by. So, yes, I wouldn't say I was starving, but I didn't have much and it did happen to be Paris, which is a tough city.

Reba: Was it easy for you to break into acting? I couldn't find that you struggled very much. Did you pay your dues?

Robert Redford: I paid them. I think it's probably because a lot of people aren't aware of what my early life was like as an actor. I didn't sit around for ten years without a job, but I paid my dues. I started in New York City, in the theater, and I went to audition after audition after audition and lost a lot of parts to someone who was better looking than I was or was politically well-known or something like that. I went to many auditions and didn't have any money and struggled like a lot of people but not for very long. Then I got into television and worked in the last of the early live days of television, and I spent a period of time doing a lot of television guest shots and then finally I got into film and in the early roles that I played, there were a lot of very different characters, crazy, psychotics, rapists, murderers—all kinds of characters that I don't think anyone's ever seen because why would they? So, it's only the latter part of your acting career that people become really aware of you so they tend to set you in that sight, that's all you've really done, therefore, it must have come easy. It didn't come easy but also didn't, it didn't come terribly hard.

Reba: When I saw the film, I saw amazing pictures that did not need words. Was it a conscious decision not to clutter it up with a lot of dialogue?

Robert Redford: Yes, that's right. You give the audience access to the soul of the situation or the soul of an animal or a human being by letting it breathe, by creating space around it for the audience to come in rather than being stopped by a word. Not that words necessarily have to stop you but either stopped by a frenzy of images that don't let you in, they just keep hitting you back and forth. They entertain you but they don't let you in. I love words and I love good words in films, but I believe it is film, after all, and there is a novel and there is film. And film is meant to tell its story essentially visually.

Reba: I have to ask this question—you're a good actor, you're a good director, what took you so long for this really good director to direct this really good actor?

Robert Redford: [laughs] Oh, to direct the actor? I don't know that it ever would have happened, quite frankly, had it not been for the circumstances around this film because it was the material in this film, the story, the characters, the condition, the situation, the uniqueness of the story and the fact that it was a love story made it a very appealing picture to direct. The role that I played was very attractive to act in, I was a different person as a director than I was as an actor. I didn't think that I'd ever want to do it, but it was only because here was a project that had both, a part I wanted to play and a story I wanted to direct, so it was kind of forced together.

Reba: But were you harder on yourself as the director directing the actor?

Robert Redford: I was in this sense that I did not have much patience with myself, the director to the actor. I didn't give the actor much time, I didn't do many takes, I was a little self-conscious. I didn't want to keep everybody waiting, you know, so I moved along quickly, and the actor did not demand much from the director [laughs].

Reba: I just wondered how you survive the fame.

Robert Redford: Well, I, uh, that's a good question, and I think it's probably, the best way to answer it is to say that I've tried to create another life for myself to go to so that I'm not completely overwhelmed by this business. I don't really much like this business. I like the art of it, but I don't care much about the business of it. And I think the way it's been possible for me to do it and to maintain some consistency with it is to realize exactly what it is. When people recognize you, they're recognizing the person on the screen and there's so much distortion that comes with that. You're presented fifteen feet high, voice booming out over and you're bigger than life on the screen, which I'm not. If you just keep in your mind that that's what people are responding to. Now that's not to say that somebody...there isn't some sort of a connection between me and the work I do on film that people might be responding to my personality or something about me. But I think a lot of it is the fact that that's a character out there that is out there and I'm here. I try to keep them separate whenever I can. When I work, there's that guy and when I'm living my life, there's this guy.

After the interview was over, Redford asked me, while still in his interview suite, with microphones on, to dinner. I declined by saying I had to get this tape interview back to Los Angeles. In reality, I would have loved to have gone, I really wasn't leaving for one more day, but the studio listens to any conversation in the TV suite. I knew if I had said yes there would be a no when it came to my next film job. All I have now was the memory that he thought I was interesting enough to spend an evening with.

23
DENZEL WASHINGTON

Glory brought Denzel Washington his first Academy Award as best supporting actor. For me, the film gave me the chance to create a video school program, which until then had only been done as print lessons. After I was given the approved print lesson plan for Glory, I pulled scenes from the film and added narration to match so that print and video were now one lesson plan. Sponsored by Eastman Kodak, the video tapes were delivered to more than 100,000 schools, which then shared the video so that millions of school children were exposed and it's still being used today when teaching about the Civil War.

Reba: Was there a moment when you knew you were going to be an actor?

Denzel Washington: I remember looking out on stage, looking out in the audience when I was at Fordham University, and going, "Boy, I really like this." I remember the first film I ever did, *Carbon Copy*, and I said to myself, "Well, this is just the natural world for me. This just feels comfortable." And so that's probably when I really said it.

Reba: That's funny. I wonder if because you were so new why you didn't get scared at acting.

Denzel Washington: I do get scared. I still get scared. With the film, you know, it kind of wears off. And most smart film directors always give the actor something light to do first or walk through, or you don't put a big heavy scene right in the beginning because you need to warm up into it and get a couple of shots in, get used to it, get a part of the rhythm in, get over your nerves, they say. And especially I've heard it said in theater if you're not nervous, it's time to get out. If you don't have those little butterflies going opening night or whatever, then it's time to quit.

Reba: Does it ever get easier for you to see yourself on screen?

Denzel Washington: I don't watch. I watch each film basically one time by myself, and I do that because I know I have to talk to the press, so I know what I'm talking about. Once I snuck into the back of a theater when we were in Philadelphia, shooting in Philadelphia, and Malcolm X came out, and that was a mistake because we drew too much attention to ourselves. And coming from theater where you don't watch your work. I don't want to lose the magic or whatever. I don't want to analyze what I'm doing. I don't work that way. I'm not a technical performer per se, so I wouldn't want to look at the film.

Reba: When you were first starting out in your career. And I thought *When the Chickens Come Home to Roost* was really kind of your first big break. Am I right?

Denzel Washington: Yeah, in a theater in New York, yes. I mean it was an off-Broadway play that we played in 150-seat theater and we had a thousand people every night trying to get in. So it was like people were coming down to see me. I met everybody doing this little play for only twenty-five dollars a week and Diana Ross would be there one night and Muhammad Ali would be then the next night. And it was like, "Well, who's this kid?" It was feeling like, well, I'm beginning to arrive in the New York theater community. And as a result of that play, in fact, I got *A Soldier's Play*, which went on to become the film. So, yeah, in a lot of ways it was. Although I had done television and one feature film before that play.

Reba: How do you hold on when you know what you want to do, but you can't get that break?

Denzel Washington: Well, you do what you gotta do until you can do what you want to do. You know, I remember after *Carbon Copy* being in the unemployment office and seeing somebody I know in the line C and they're like, "What are you doing in here, man? I just see you starring in a movie. What are you doing?" I'm like, "I'm here getting my $126, and whatever it was, and 50 cents. I'm waiting to get the line B like you are," a humbling experience.

Reba: You never forgot it though. I heard…

Denzel Washington: I still have my book was that you were getting ready to say. Yeah, I still got my unemployment books, yeah. My wife and I, we both have ours. I remember me giving her the seventy-five cents to get downtown for auditions and she had to figure out how to get home and I had to sneak on both ways to just eat somewhere and if you cannot find something to eat you invite yourself to somebody's house.

Reba: I guess what's happening now is really nice because it validates the dreams that you had to hold out and do the kind of roles that you wanted to come true.

Denzel Washington: The one thing I'm the happiest about in terms of my career is the fact that I got there by the grace of God, first of all, but short of that, I got there just by working hard, not partying with the right people, not compromising myself in any way or cutting any kind of deals, just by working hard, just by plugging along, sowing wood, as I like to call it. You know, I'm a twenty-year overnight sensation.

Reba: Also, the last five roles or six roles that you've played, it didn't matter what you look like, what color or ethnicity you are. Do you think there's a change happening in Hollywood or is it just you?

Denzel Washington: I think there is a change. I think that it's maybe just a testament to me moving up the ladder due to my ability. There were people that were willing to take what some might consider to be a risk, like a Julia Roberts who said she wanted me to play the part and the studio didn't, but she did? And she said, I think he'd be good for the part, and $200 million later everybody's happy. So, she took a chance there, and it could be argued that Jonathan Demme did too. But I like to think that you know, yes, the best actor should get the part or the actor that's right for the part should get the part, but it is a business. If Joe, who is a great actor, but nobody's seen him, and Tom Cruise, who is a great actor, but everybody knows him, you know, everybody's going to want to choose Tom Cruise.

Reba: I know I've gotten a wrap; I'll have to ask you one question. You're famous now. I just want to know how fame has affected you and how you can keep it simple.

Denzel Washington: It's just day in and day out. It seems to affect other people more than it affects me. I mean, just do the things I do every other day. How do I deal with fame? By putting out the garbage.

In this interview when Washington mentioned Julia Roberts, it was for the film *The Pelican Brief.* Roberts had told the studio, Warner Bros., that she would not do the film unless Denzel Washington was her leading man. The problem was that there was sexual tension in the script, and they were afraid that American audiences were not ready for it. This was the first time Washington had had a white costar. The compromise was to remove the one scene where they kissed. He didn't kiss a white costar until the film *Flight* in 2012.

Before our interview started, I asked him what movies and actors inspired him. He told me that in the mid-seventies when he was just starting out, there weren't any black movie stars other than Sidney Poitier and some comedians like Richard Pryor, so he assumed his career would be in the theater.

When I sat down with Washington for *Remember the Titans,* I explained that the studio wanted no mention of high school football for the international release and we both laughed. I selected a few sound bites from this interview.

Reba: Did anybody clue you in to how much rejection there is in the acting business?

Denzel Washington: Ignorance is bliss. You know, I was a junior in college and I started acting and I sorta stumbled right into a leading role right from the start. So I got a lot of positive feedback right from the beginning. I really didn't know anything about Hollywood or making movies and to be quite honest, we were sort of snobbish right here at Lincoln Center in New York. We were going to play the great roles and maybe one day make $600 a week on Broadway. I mean, that's as far as I could see; just to find something that I was good at and that I enjoy doing was enough for me at that time. So no, to answer your question, there wasn't any pressure until I had to start making a living at it. You know, the pressure of paying the rent.

Reba: You set it up for me. You are a movie star. Any pressure now?

Denzel Washington: I like to think of it like this. I'm a more popular actor than I used to be. I still consider myself an actor. I acted in movies and, and you know, I think that if you don't deliver, you know that people will let you know.

Reba: Can you do the Dad things?

Denzel Washington: Oh, absolutely. Yeah. I coach. Yeah. I'm a father first. I don't get life mixed up with making a living. I was there for all four of my children being born. When the first one was born, I recognize the difference between life and making a living. You know, my family is life; acting is making a living.

Walt Disney records released a seven-minutes score from *Remember the Titans* composed by musician Trevor Rabin. The track called "Titans Spirit" has been used on numerous sporting telecasts, particularly the closing credits for the Olympic games from 2002 to 2016. It was also used after future president Barack Obama's speech at the 2008 Democratic National Convention and was immediately used following his victory speech upon winning the 2008 presidential election.

The best story that came out of this film happened at a premier in Washington, DC. President Clinton arrived unannounced and invited Denzel to join him at the White House. Denzel refused; he was not staying to see the film as he was flying to New York to surprise his wife on her birthday. Perhaps that's why he is still married.

24
TOM HANKS

I got a call from Universal to do an interview with Tom Hanks for the 1986 release of the film The Money Pit. This was not an ordinary job, as the video publicity had already been done; this was for the press junket. Hanks was in a remote part of Israel, on the film Every Time We Say Goodbye, and could not be hooked up for a satellite interview, so my raw interview was given to the journalists on the junket.

As it was early in his career, Hanks didn't dress up; he just wore a plaid flannel work shirt, no makeup, and messy hair. He was very candid, funny, and generous—in fact, he didn't realize he was even being funny with one of his comments, which I never forgot: "I look like a squirrel on top of a motorcycle," he said when describing his movie star persona looks. I knew what it meant because I knew that he did not have classic movie star good looks. I was so disappointed when the raw interview went missing that I decided to share some sound bites from this early interview that had been produced for my cruise lectures. I hope that the interview, which was misplaced, will reappear someday. Later, I had the opportunity to interview him again for Toy Story, That Thing You Do, and Toy Story 2, and he just doesn't disappoint.

Reba: Why acting? Did you think you would end up in Hollywood?

Tom Hanks: When I was acting in high school, I never thought I'd act after high school. I was lucky enough to figure out that I couldn't do anything else right about the time they started paying me to act. I had no knowledge of what it was I wanted to do. I was just kind of wandering around. I wanted to goof off as much as possible and now I get paid to do that.

Reba: Did you move a lot as a kid?

Tom Hanks: It was the greatest preparation for being an actor as possible; this kind of nomadic lifestyle that I led as a kid, moving around a lot too, to a point now there might be some deep psychological scars because I can't stay in any one place for more than about eighteen months. But it used to be only six months I could only stay in a place, so it's getting better now.

Reba: How difficult is doing animated comedy like Toy Story?

Tom Hanks: And it is very hard, the famous line "dying is easy, comedy is hard." But I think what makes it so difficult is that there are no shades of gray for the most part. You make the movie, you put it up on the screen, people either laugh or they don't. If they laugh, you've done your job and you can reap those rewards and benefits. And if they don't laugh, you have failed miserably. You will never work again, and they will railroad you out of town on a rail and then send you back to the Quad Cities. Being in an animated movie is absolutely, completely, totally beyond me. Now, I had talked to other people who had been voices and some that had appeared in even a Disney films. In fact, I had met Matthew Broderick right about the time that we were going to begin doing this. And I said, "So what's that like?" And he gave me a description of, "Well, you sort of, say your line, and then a bunch of people behind glass talk about it, and you can't hear them and then they may pose and they think about and they press a button, and then they tell you to do it all over again but in a slightly different way." And that is exactly what it's like in order to be acting in an animated movie.

Reba: How much of you goes into your characters?

Tom Hanks: Well, I think that's the reason that I'm attracted to the roles in the first place is that I think they do...I mean, they do land on me in some way that I can recognize, maybe not in a big way, but still there's some aspect of who they are and what they're go-ing through that I can relate to somehow via my own life, or my own—my own experience. I can be just as volatile, and I've yelled just as much, and I've been as just as threatened in the course of my own life. But I don't think I can take a job without having some sort of innate kind of very natural, very instinctive kind of relation-ship to the character and what he's going through. That's the thing that makes it so easy to say yes to these jobs. It's hard when it is so artificial and so far removed. It's hard then to say, "Well, I can do that." I end up saying no to movies more often, because it's, "Look, I haven't a clue. I don't have the slightest idea how to approach this. It would take me years in order to be able to prepare for this."

Reba: I just wondered if in the end the roles were so diverse, is it unfair to ask if you have a favorite?

Tom Hanks: Well, I don't have a favorite role. If I could go back and say, I'd like to have made this section of this movie forever. You know, I could have laid in that command module on *Apollo 13* for weeks and been very, very happy. I could have been in Viet-nam with Forrest Gump for a real long time, and I think I would have—would have enjoyed that. I could have danced with Antonio Banderas for days and days and been very happy in Philadelphia. And I would have loved to have been able to actually play base-ball for a lot longer time that I got to on *A League of Their Own*. So, the roles themselves are all far too special and far too divergent, really. I couldn't choose one between the other as being a favorite. But I do remember moments of making almost every movie where I thought, you know what, I could have lingered there for much longer time.

Reba: But have you gotten to a point now where you sleep well at night, knowing that you've really proven who Tom Hanks is?

Tom Hanks: Well, I have to say that the two Academy Awards really do lift something of a burden from my shoulders, which is actu-ally kind of scary, because then I think, well, does that mean I'm going to have the same drive instinctively that, that brought me to those roles in the first place and maybe execute them however it is that we executed them in order to do that? So right then out of this great thing, out of the sense of relief, comes a sense of dread, a sense of worry. So, I think that all actors are screwed up and neurotic to a degree and so that even they can take something as good as that and turn it into some sort of thing that has to be dealt with.

Reba: I was fortunate enough to interview Jimmy Stewart ten years ago, and I asked him what would he like to be known as, an actor or a movie star. And I wonder if you'll answer the same question.

Tom Hanks: Oh, well, I'd much rather be known as—I know I am a movie star. I would—I would much rather be known as being an actor though. Movie stars are these guys who have autographs and security people who get whisked in and out of the back rooms of hotels and on airplanes. But I think I would be very happy if people, you know, years from now, are looking at my performances and saying, "Man, that guy could do anything." That would really make me happy.

Recently I talked to Tom Hanks at a party for his latest film *A Beautiful Day in the Neighborhood* and told him about the book and the interview and with a smile I got his approval.

I was really looking forward to interviewing Whitney Houston for the film *Waiting to Exhale*. *Waiting to Exhale* was the first film where I was assigned to interview her, but she left without doing anything for the international marketplace. But I got to interview Angela Bassett, Loretta Devine, and Lela Rochon and the bonus was director Forest Whitaker.

I was really devastated she had skipped doing my interview. Her actions upset the studio, but they did nothing to stop her. I produced a video profile of Houston from the electronic press kit raw footage provided by the studio and loaded it with behind-the-scenes footage and movie clips to cover a weak interview.

When it came time for me to interview Whitney Houston for *The Preacher's Wife,* I was surprised when the publicist handling the press junket for the film called telling me to come over to the interview suite now. I was put in immediately a day early and excited to actually be sitting across from Houston. I would not do my Denzel Washington interview until the following day, but I was not worried he would bail. Washington had a lot invested in this film as his production company developed the project. The role of Julia was written with Houston in mind and it took a while for her to see the parallels between her own life and her love of gospel music and the character she would play. The topic of conversation among the journalists the night before the junket were the rumors of her continued drug use. I walked into her suite and could not get over how beautiful, healthy, and composed she looked.

Reba: You've been singing your whole life; do you think you missed anything growing up because you're always performing?

Whitney Houston: No, I don't. I think that there's a portion of my life that my mother had full control over until I was about eighteen because it was like my mother said, I couldn't sign a contract unless I graduated high school, so, therefore, those years were spent in high school. I was singing and working on the weekends and modeling and stuff like that, but I couldn't do a full-time thing until I graduated high school. And then after that I probably missed like young womanhood, like when women are out like a twenty-one, twenty-two, twenty-three, twenty-four and out partying and having a good time and meeting guys, stuff like that, I was on the road working.

Reba: It looked like your life was perfect.

Whitney Houston: Far from it.

Reba: But you have a daughter now. Would you let her, if she was you, do the things your mother let you do or didn't do?

Whitney Houston: Yeah, I would, my mother had a pretty good rein on me. You know what I'm saying? When you're raised in church and you're raised in the background of God-fearing religion and it's instilled in you, there's a certain boundary that you don't cross. You know what I'm saying? You know, like, I could have gotten into a lot more trouble than I got into if I hadn't thought about, "Oh, my mother's going to kill me," or "My father and my mother is going to be so disappointed. I know God's watching me." You know what I'm saying? Stuff like that.

Reba: The gospel music, what kind of memories did it bring back?

Whitney Houston: The memories of singing in church are ones that I cherish most because it wasn't worldly. It was fresh. It wasn't stale, it didn't get repetitious. It was expressive. Singing Gospel was energy and a passion and a love for the creator. And that's a good memory for me.

Reba: Do you think a person can make a difference?

Whitney Houston: Sure.

Reba: You tell me.

Whitney Houston: Sure. I mean, you know, for myself. You have to really try to remember the important things and put them in their priorities, perspective places. And anybody can be an angel when you want to give from your heart, and you want to help people who are in need.

Reba: Has anybody ever given to you and been like an angel?

Whitney Houston: Yes, there have been angels in my life. The first angel I ever remember was my mother being my angel. She was so unselfish. She sacrificed and she taught me everything that she knew about life and about music.

Reba: But did she prepare you for fame?

Whitney Houston: Yes, she did—as best she could. There's some stuff you can't teach a child; they'd have to go through it.

Reba: This is probably a very, very unfair question, and don't hit me, I'm a lady. But how much has success changed you? How different are you?

Whitney Houston: Probably a lot more paranoid. Success doesn't change you, fame does. You got a whole world of people calling your name and you really don't know them. It's weird.

Reba: One of the things that got me was the theme of the movie of hope and love. When you're working on a film like this and you walk off the set at the end, what do you take with you? What did it leave you with that?

Whitney Houston: That you can make a difference. You can. There are Julias and Henrys and Dudleys and Jeremiahs, and Marguerites, you know, these are real people, they don't—they don't seem imaginaryto me like they're made up or like it's a fairy tale. It seems like it's quite real to me.

Reba: I'm from the outside and I look in and I think that you live a life that's like a fairy-tale, but I bet in reality even though it looks gorgeous, you probably have down days just as well as everybody. How do you deal with them? Would you allow yourself to?

Whitney Houston: There is a misconception of the fact that when we become famous that we have these beautiful, perfect lives and that nothing is ever on a low. It's a bad conception because then people always think that you have to be this grand old person that's just happy about life and everything. Because what, we got money? Money doesn't make you happy. It never did. I mean, history will tell you that. And fame certainly doesn't make you happy. People will tell you that who are famous. You've got to find the happiness in yourself. You've got to know who you are before you step into this business because if you're trying to find it, you'll probably wind up being somebody else that you probably don't even like. I like me because I love God so much and He is first in my life before anything. He's first and I'm glad about that because I know I can depend on Him. He never changes, stays the same. He's love.

Reba: I like you too.

Whitney Houston: Thank you.

During this interview she came close to lifting the veil, ever so slightly, between who she was and what her public persona was. I believed she has had a difficult time separating Whitney Houston the performer—whose voice will be remembered in millions of weddings, thousands of karaoke sessions, and just about half of all television vocal show auditions—from Whitney Houston the wife and mother. It must be difficult for a famous woman like Houston to not be aware of her presence, but she seemed uncomfortable with her fame.

I really liked her, and she made me feel like she was beinghonest with me, but addicts can be deceiving. I am an addict—my drug of choice was sugar, which I control now—but I am in a twelve-step program where I have been able to deal with the painful problems it caused me beyond the weight gain. I have kept sixty pounds off for over twenty years. Whitney Houston had everything, even rehab, and she squandered everything—her talent and her life

When Whitney Houston died, I was getting ready to board a cruise ship where I would lecture about my Hollywood career, including an excerpt from the only interview I ever did with her. I must admit that I felt sad even though I had only spent six minutes with her. But she had really left an impression on me. The video profile I did on her in 1996 got played over and over again when she died and is still played whenever a story comes out about her or her family.

I was surprised to get an email ten years later from a woman in Australia looking for Houston interview footage for a documentary. I was thrilled beyond words when portions of this interview were used in the finished documentary *Can I Be Me*, directed by Nick Broomfield. The documentary sifts through the details of Whitney Houston's sad, secret life, and I was lucky to have captured a small part of it.

26
JOHN TRAVOLTA

John Travolta's career turned around with films like Pulp Fiction, Get Shorty, White Man's Burden, and Michael. He gained international attention when dancing with Diana, Princess of Wales, at the White House. In fact, that picture of him dancing not only went around the world but so did the dress that Diana was wearing, which was named the "Travolta dress."

Sitting down with John Travolta for the film *Broken Arrow*—where he played a stealth pilot with an agenda—I knew all about his career, but I wanted to know about the man. Travolta rose to fame during the seventies with *Welcome Back, Kotter.* His real success came with *Saturday Night Fever*, and even got an Oscar nomination for the film. He rode that success to *Grease*, where he played a high school student—a sexy one—when he was twenty-three. He was still going strong in the eighties with *Urban Cowboy*, and then his career took a downturn. I knew I could open the interview in a comfortable way, but I really wanted to find out what made him tick when things were not great. I used this interview to try to find out how he looked at life when it wasn't perfect.

Reba: Pilots seem very calm when they're in the cockpit. Does it also give you a sense of control? And when you play a pilot as a pilot, how accurate was this?

John Travolta: That aspect of it I thought was completely accurate. I think that pilots by nature are well trained in their field and therefore there is a calmness in the cockpit. In case there is an emergency, you have all your faculties about you.

Reba: Does that calmness carry over when you get on the ground? Is it now part of your life?

John Travolta: I would say that in the cockpit, you're very specifically extroverted onto your instruments. But in your life, you have to deal continually with personalities. You can in the cockpit as well if you have the right personality right next to you. But I think that it varies a little more. It's more of an obstacle course in life versus in the cockpit.

Reba: Is it a different kind of success than what you had earlier?

John Travolta: Yes.

Reba: In what way?

John Travolta: The difference in the success now is that there is more varied types of products that are offered to me with more interesting directors, and opportunities for me to show different sides of what I can do. And not that that wasn't always the case; it's just that as this particular round seems to afford me that, which I'm pretty excited about.

Reba: But you never gave up, and I wondered why. It's so much easier to walk away when things aren't the way you want it.

John Travolta: I think because I was viewing it. I didn't view it so dismally. I viewed it as, "Gee, they're still hiring me for movies, and I'm getting paid fairly well." And it may not be the best and it may not be the greatest situation, but I fared pretty well with it here. But another looking at me with a different viewpoint might have looked at it differently. And it's a revelation to find out how varied people's view of it was.

Reba: So, you never get down, do you?

John Travolta: Not too much, no.

Reba: And this is probably terrible to ask. How much fun is it to be a movie star?

John Travolta: Well, I'd imagine if you were me, it'd be pretty fun. I'd imagine others might interpret their stardom with a mixed bag of feelings. But I enjoy…I think of life as an art form. I live art as life. I live life as an art form. Whether it's flying a plane, or eating a dinner, or experiencing a movie, I just think that happiness is kind of within you to create the right effects on yourself.

Reba: And if you weren't making movies, do you have any idea what you'd do—besides flying a plane? That's not fair.

John Travolta: Oh, boy. Well, I'd probably be in something where I got to travel because I like travel, probably in that field somehow.

What you can't see when you read his interview was his body language, which was loose until I asked about his career downturn. He sat with his arms crossed once I asked about that, and he did not uncross them until I asked about the movie again.

I knew later in the year that John Travolta and I would meet again for *Phenomenon* and I would have to go in a similar but slightly different direction for this interview. I never thought that any of these interviews would see light of day as some questions I like to ask more than once. When I saw him again, I realized he remembered me, but I had hoped not all my questions. I was a pushover for fantasy in the movies with or without romance and so I liked this film and let him know it right off the bat. His character, George, got hit by a white light and became a genius. He developed an ability to retain information, move objects with his mind, and, best of all, never needed to sleep. I looked up psychokinesis and discovered that it's not a verified phenomenon, which made me realize how clever the screenwriter for this film was. Travolta's body language during this interview was different than *Broken Arrow*. He was uncomfortable with the latter when he sat with his arms crossed at his chest. I could tell that he felt comfortable with my questions this time, so I pushed a little to get some answers. This little quirky film also made over one hundred and fifty million dollars, and the world knew John Travolta was back in business.

Reba: Thank you. You started working when you were twelve. And I wonder now that you're a man of a certain age, you ever felt you missed anything? Or if you've been in a really wonderful merry-go- round in life?

John Travolta: Well, I feel like I've been in a really wonderful merry- go-round. It's had its ups and downs, but I've dealt with them pretty well. I probably only missed the street savvy that people get when they're out in the world and they learn to protect themselves a little bit more and trust appropriate times, a little bit less, you know. Sort of that, I feel like I've enjoyed my journey.

Reba: It's really funny, last week, I asked my husband if all his dreams had come true. And he said no. And he said to me, "Have all your dreams come true?" And I said better than I ever thought they would. And I wonder if your wife asked you that question? Did your dreams come true?

John Travolta: Every dream of mine has come true. And I'm with you, probably more than expected. I'm living in somebody else's novel. I have a few novels that are going on actually.

Reba: So , there's, well then maybe I should ask you this? What is it that you can't do? You write, you fly, you act, and you get awards. Well, what's left?

John Travolta: I have no control over my agent. He's a madman. Once he gets his hooks in me, he is going to come over here and grab me up. No, I don't know how to answer that. It's a compliment that you're giving me and I thank you for it. And it's more that there are so many things that I want to do even beyond that, that I should maybe stop and smell the roses and realize that everything that you've said is true. And now I should appreciate that and go from that point.

Reba: In this film, and because this film to me was very different than the last films I've seen you in—and I'll make this the last question— what are you going to take away? I have a feeling there's something from this film that you're going to put like an inside pocket close to your soul. And I wondered if you share something that George instilled in you.

John Travolta: George confirmed in my personality the urge that I have to take care everyone I love, and then make sure they're all right before I go, and to take full responsibility. And I can honestly say I'm somewhat selfless in that and I try to be like George in that way, you know?

Most of the world knew about Travolta's practice of Scientology, a subject I never brought up with him. I got a call from two members of Scientology to meet at their Hollywood center to discuss a Travolta film. The two men I met with wanted me to produce an electronic press kit for *Battlefield Earth*, which would be shooting in Montreal. They thought I would waive my fee for the honor of working on an L. Ron Hubbard and John Travolta film. I didn't have to think twice before declining. Before I left the building, I went to the ladies' bathroom, as I was curious to see it. I was not disappointed. It was very elegant with a lot of crystal, marble, and gold fixtures.

Another year, another John Travolta movie. In fact, *Ladder 49* was my fifth interview with him. His latest film touched me deeply as I was from Baltimore, Maryland, where the film was set and my husband and I lived through the Malibu fire of 1993. This press junket started off in a strange way when I was told not to expect to get any kind of interview with Joaquin Phoenix. Earlier in the day a journalist on the junket, thinking he was clever, asked Phoenix if called 911 when his brother River was dying from an overdose. I had no idea when I went to Joaquin Phoenix's suite hoping that he could, with some prompting, actually a lot of prompting, remember our conversation at the Cannes Film Festival and give me a usable interview. I got a longer interview than anyone expected, which surprised Joaquin, the studio, and me. I knew that Travolta's interview would ultimately carry more weight when promoting the film.

Reba: What about you? Is it unfair to ask a big movie star if he's afraid of fire? I don't know.

John Travolta: No, I was more afraid of the training, not the fire, because the training demanded much more. See, with fire you usually have the equipment to, if you're a firefighter, to fight it. So that's not the frightening part. The frightening part is the situations that one could get put into, for instance, getting trapped. That's much more claustrophobic, much more complicated, because how to get out. The other thing would be catapulting yourself off the side of a building with a rope, you know, that's a situation and that's not something that, you know, you get the idea it's not so much the literal fire as much as what does the fire…situations the fire put you in?

Reba: You've had so much of your life in the public eye. Are you used to it? So, you've been famous your whole life?

John Travolta: Mostly.

Reba: How intrusive do you find it?

John Travolta: I think, like anything that happens in your whole life, you get used to it. And so, therefore, I don't look at it as intrusiveness as much as part of what is my normal life. So, you know, I'm a sentient person. I respond to interruptions or respond to compliments and I respond to, you know, anything the way a sentient person would. So, it's not that complicated for me really. I mean, I don't want to make it look like it's something really.

Reba: Well, good, then I'll ask you about December 7, 1977. You remember that night? The night of the premiere?

John Travolta: *Saturday Night Fever*.

Reba: It's the beginning of John Travolta explosion. Did you know it when you did it?

John Travolta: Oh, no. *Saturday Night Fever* was a movie that we thought was an art film. Like an indie film, you know, I mean, it was not looked at as a…I thought that I was correctly portraying a slice of life that would just be interesting to watch, you know. I didn't really think of it as anything that would change the face of the earth. And it did it almost unbeknownst to me.

Reba: So, the best thing I can do is, what's the best thing about acting? You get to be all these people or is it something else?

John Travolta: It's all of that. You get to be…you get a respite from yourself; you get to be someone else, which is kind of fun. You get to create all the time different, you know; the craft of acting is something that I really liked, too. I like discovering how a person walks and talks and speaks and eats and smokes and emotes and I like all the minutiae of, of acting. You know, it's part of the fun of it.

Reba: Your films have been extraordinary. And I just wonder in looking back, because we're coming from a high, real high point. How did you deal with the valleys? We know how to deal with the peaks. How did you deal with the valleys? Because it's a good piece of advice you could give us?

John Travolta: Well, if you don't look at them as valleys but look at them as learning experiences. And again, life is a new today, don't regret yesterday. What can you do about it other than learn from it? And you always create your tomorrows, that's what life is about.

In 2018, I was contacted by Russian television known in LA as RT. They wanted me to do a monthly interview segment where I would discuss nasty stories about famous people. The first actor they wanted was John Travolta and the different lawsuits that he was involved in with men. I couldn't do it. I have no feelings about John Travolta, good or bad, but it's not my style and it made me uncomfortable. They never called me again.

27
BEN AFFLECK

I don't always get the movies or the film stars I want because I have to be hired for video publicity. For years, I had watched Ben Affleck's movies but really fell in love with him when I saw him win an Oscar for best screenplay with Matt Damon for *Goodwill Hunting*. I had to wait for Affleck's *Armageddon* in 1998 to actually interview him on the international press junket.

The film starred Bruce Willis, who was not happy to be there, so he left as early as he could. My interview with Willis was just terrible and my editor produced a remarkable profile by using very little of the star and lots of film footage. Willis's behavior affected everyone, including Ben Affleck, who told his publicist that he was leaving too. My interviews were being played on thousands of televisions shows worldwide, so I panicked as I had interviewed everyone but Ben Affleck. On every job that I did for Buena Vista International I was accompanied by a studio executive, which I thought was to make sure I didn't cause any problems. The reality was when something went wrong, the studio executive was there to troubleshoot the problem. When Affleck also wanted to leave, my studio executive really went into action. Privately she went to him and explained how important his interview was for the film and Jerry Bruckheimer, the producer. Whatever she did, he smiled and said of course I will do this. I was hyperventilating when I went to interview Affleck because I was upset and disappointed with Bruce Willis and his interview. I knew that Ben Affleck was hot, and his interview would garner a lot of airplay. I walked into the room to find a very happy young man who told me to "stay as long as you want, ask anything you want, and we will have a good time." I took a deep breath—actually I took a few deep breaths—and preceded to have fun with this charming young man.

Armageddon was a science fiction disaster film directed by Michael Bay and produced by Jerry Bruckheimer. Both were known to deliver blockbuster films that cost a lot of money and made a lot of money. The film follows a group of blue-collar deep core drillers sent by NASA to stop a gigantic asteroid on a collision course with earth. There are no secrets in Hollywood; two months before I did the interviews the studio spent three million dollars to create new special effects scenes. This additional footage was specifically added for the television advertising campaign. The studio wanted *Armageddon* to be the counter film to *Deep Impact*, which was released in May with pretty good reviews. They were similar and Disney needed to make an impact of their own when they released *Armageddon* in July. Interestingly enough, *Deep Impact* made more money at three hundred and fifty million dollars worldwide because their budget was much smaller. *Armageddon* received four Academy Award nominations, but the only acting award the film got was for Bruce Willis, who won a Razzie for worst actor. Now I know why Willis didn't want to promote the movie. The film had mostly negative reviews but was an international sensation becoming the highest grossing film of 1998, earning over five hundred million dollars.

Reba: Ready? Okay. How did you know you wanted to be an actor? Because you look like a basketball player?

Ben Affleck: I may look like a basketball player, but I knew I wanted to be an at a actor pretty young age. I was cast in an independent film when I was seven years old by friend of my mom—put a little kid. I ran around the New England Aquarium. I had a scene where I was sleeping. I had another scene where I rattled off a few lines, but I had so much fun that I was sort of end up mimicking all the other adult actors, because what I wasn't accustomed to is they repeat their lines so many times so I get to memorize everyone else's lines that I would go around imitating them. And consequently, they asked me to come in and audition. That guy's wife was casting a TV series that was doing a nationwide search. I got that part. And then I started going from Boston to New York auditioning, and it was the only thing really that I ever felt entirely comfortable doing. And the only thing that I could get paid for that didn't feel like work. You know what I mean?

Reba: You're actually funny at that; you're not even saying that you were scared. I'm really surprised. I guess. Maybe being young...

Ben Affleck: Scared? What do you think I would be scared of? Failure?

Reba: Standing up in front of strangers and doing something.

Ben Affleck: I got nervous from time to time. I occasionally got nervous. The more publicity you do and the more this kind of appearances and stuff you do, the more you get accustomed to talking in front of people and going on talk shows and you get sort of accustomed to performing. I don't think you ever are entirely at ease. And if you are, it probably means that you lost a little bit of edge or something. But I think ultimately being relaxed is sort of half the battle to acting. If you're nervous, it infects everything you're doing, and if you're not at ease as an actor, you know, you can't really play a character; you'll always be in some measure yourself.

Reba: You went to the Academy Awards with your mother. What advice did she give you?

Ben Affleck: My mother has given me more advice ranging from the tried and true Polonius to, you know, "To thine own self be true." "Neither a borrower nor lender be," stuff like that. She's also advised me not to go out with women with false breasts, she's advised me all manner of things, you know, she was pointing out people at the Academy Awards that look like nice people and people she thought looked like bad people. She's advised me to have children as soon as humanly possible. She's advised me to take care of my mother who nearly died in labor having me, and I try to follow all of that advice, especially the latter.

Reba: Now is there anything clean that you could tell me that went on behind the scenes, especially any of the love scenes?

Ben Affleck: Well, for one thing, in the love scene with the animal crackers in Armageddon, it was ice cold and they made Liv, you know, has to lay on her back, and I'm moving this animal cracker on her stomach, and Michael, the director, is fixated on exactly the way the animal cracker was supposed to look and he was torturing us. I mean, it was freezing cold. We had these enormous heaters blasting at us. It was frigid. And then finally, you know, he was like, he made me pick her up and swing around and he kept doing coverage. And I find that I mean, Liv was so shivering, and our lips were blue that I just lost it. And I was like, "Michael, you're insane. You're going to kill us of pneumonia." And he just, like, burst out laughing, he's like, "Roll in the puddle," because the last thing you want to do is roll around in the water. And it wasn't like water they had put there, it was just a puddle. And I was like, "No, we're not going to puddle. Are you out of your mind?" And the truth is, he is a little bit out of his mind. But I think that's part of what makes him pretty talented guy.

Reba: What's the best thing about acting?

Ben Affleck: The best thing about acting if you can be successful is that it affords you the opportunity to—it affords you some extraordinary access to places that you'd never otherwise would be granted access to. For me, like places like NASA, the Johnson and Kennedy Space Centers. It also affords you the opportunity to be self-indulgent, to have fun for a living, to be creative for a living, which is a real luxury. Most people feel like their work is a grind. They work in an office; they twist wrenches or a lift boxes and it's just done for money to put food on the table. Whereas if you can get paid to be an actor it's an enormous luxury because it means that you're doing something that you have fun doing.

Reba: Before they kill me. I'm sorry, I've got to ask you. This is the flip side. You pay a price for that, it's called fame. Your life has got to have changed from that little boy at seven. How do you deal with that?

Ben Affleck: Your life changes significantly once you're in movies that people see. The way that I deal with that is by trying not to think about it. And by trying to ignore it more or less and continue to just be sort of the person I am and make decisions not based on considerations that have anything to do with fame or movies or money or any of that, which I think is illusory and false and grotesque and hideous, but rather to make determinations based on, like, what my mother told me, "to thine own self be true," which I think was supposed to be a sort of hypocritical but my mother thinks is the most valuable advice you can have. In other words, just do things that you feel intuitively right. Try to be good to people. Think about other people, be considerate, share, be caring, stand by your principles and believe in yourself and take care of the people whom you love, and other than that the rest will sort of fall into place.

What I didn't know at the time was mega-million-dollar producer Jerry Bruckheimer had to convince the director, Michael Bay, that Ben Affleck would be a star. The actor was required to lose weight, get a suntan and have his teeth capped. And when the film was released the producer was absolutely right because it established Affleck as a viable leading man for Hollywood studio films. One of the reviewers described Ben Affleck as having "sexy Paul Newman charm," clearly bound for stardom.

I am very lucky to have had a job where I can be a fan, do interviews, and get paid for it. This was a perfect career path for me as I loved movies and the actors in them. By 1998, I was working for 20th Century Fox International, Buena Vista International, and Sony International, supplying more than sixty countries and close to 5,000 TV shows with my profiles and television specials. I got a chance to interview Anthony Hopkins for two studios in a short period of time. I didn't expect him to remember me, and he didn't, but I never forgot him. My first encounter with Anthony Hopkins was for the film *Mask of Zorro*, where I was hired by Sony to produce a half-hour special to introduce Antonio Banderas to the world as a romantic action hero. Hopkins played his father and his scenes included wielding a powerful whip and dashing sword play. My job was only to get him to tell me about using them, so I tried to break the ice with a little generic hero stuff. He was gruff and made fun of my questions and once I realized I got what I needed I cut the interview short. This was a first for me being miserable doing something I loved. As I was leaving the hotel, I was stopped by Anthony Hopkins's personal publicists, who apologized, stating that Mr. Hopkins had not had his morning tea. Anthony Hopkins has been very public about being a recovering alcoholic—what he needed was a sugar fix.

Some of the movies I worked on in 1998 ran the gamut from *The Parent Trap* with Lindsay Lohan to *The X Flies* with David Duchovny and Gillian Anderson. Charlize Theron in *Mighty Joe Young*, she answered me honestly when I asked her if her looks get in the way when going for a role. Her answer: "yes." Once again, another Nick Cage film, *Snake Eyes*, directed by Brian De Palma.

The biggest surprise of 1998 was when I got to interview Tim Robbins for the film *Nothing to Lose*. His publicist, Nancy, had blackballed me after the Sean Connery–James Bond issue. But again, it was Buena Vista International that wanted me. The movie was so bad, they needed me. I was sent to do interviews at the Toronto Film Festival, and I loved it because I got to see lots of movies and meet the stars.

It was a year filled with highs and lows. The highs being the three half-hour television specials I produced for the films *Replacement Killers* directed by Antoine Fuqua for Sony; *Hope Floats* starring Sandra Bullock for Fox; and *The Ringmaster*—a fictional take on *The Jerry Springer Show*—for Artisan Entertainment. I got to interview Jerry Springer, who essentially played himself. While he might be a clever talk show host, he should leave acting to the pros. The low was my last job for 20th Century Fox International after finishing *The Thin Red Line* profiles. The interviews that I did for that film were in my Oprah style and had very little about the movie and more about the actors. When I am asked to produce a special, of course my questions are different than my profile ones.

I had worked for Fox for seven years, and if I could have just kept my mouth shut, I could have worked another seven. I was asked by Hillary Clark, vice president of publicity, to turn over my interview footage from *The Thin Red Line* to a competitor for them to do the half-hour special. I didn't want to turn the footage over and begged to at least bid on a proposal. I talked too much. I didn't take no for an answer and asked again, reminding Clark that we had replaced the company she had asked me to turn my tapes over to. That was the final nail in my Fox coffin. Fox International was the first company that gave me the chance to try my video profiles internationally and I will never forget the door it opened for my career. That's my Hollywood story and I am embarrassed to tell it. Years later, when I had a radio talk show, I interviewed Hillary Clark and never brought up her firing me, which, of course, I never forgot. In fact, on that weekly show I managed to interview everyone who had given me work or fired me or took my money. It was a great cathartic experience, and I am glad that I did it

My next encounter with Anthony Hopkins was for *Instinct*, a psychological thriller. As I was sitting with other journalists waiting for my interview, a young assistant came into the holding room and asked for some cookies for Anthony Hopkins. Since Disney was giving me every live-action film for their international video publicity, everybody knew me. I immediately went to the studio executive that was asked about the cookies and said please give him cookies before I go into his interview suite, to avoid the same situation as last time. They must have because this time he answered everything and was nice too. I did not mention that I interviewed him a few months earlier and he did not remember me—a win for both of us.

Reba: I wonder, especially after this movie, if you trust your instincts and do you live by them?

Anthony Hopkins: Yeah, I do. I do know instinct is a very powerful word. It's written, and I live by my intuition more so now than going on instinct. Instinct is a very primitive action, but intuition is what I trust. It's taken me in the recent years enough fortitude and faith and courage to let go of my thinking abilities, not that they were that pristine, but to stop analyzing and making a big dog's dinner of everything in my brain and trust more. For example, I've been asked, why did you take this? Why did you accept this part? I didn't know. My intuition would tell me, "Well, it's a good story. It's an interesting story. There's quite a bit to say in it. Is this a part I can play? Yeah, it's pretty close to me. What's the director like? Is he good? Does he have an instinct about him or an intuition?" And so, I put it all together and usually end up in a pretty good situation.

Reba: Are you surprised at the gift you've been given and it's the second-time-around gift? Not many people get them! I got it. So, I really know how much it means to be able to succeed...

Anthony Hopkins: Second time around?

Reba: Yes, you had a great career, you won Emmys and then you hit the movies and you never stopped running? I think that's amazing.

Anthony Hopkins: I'm amazed. I'm more surprised than anyone, I think. Yeah, I know what you mean. I started off years ago as an actor working in the theater in England. And I always wanted to be in movies. And the first movie I got into was *The Lion in the Winter* with Katharine Hepburn and Peter O'Toole, which was not bad to end up with those two and their son. And I enjoyed it so much, I thought, "Well, hope I can do more of this." And I had a secret burning ambition to be in movies, and I wanted to come to America and live and work. And all these things worked out, and I had what they would call a respectable career, then went back to England, worked in the theater for a few years, national theater. And then *Silence of the Lambs* came along out of nowhere, and I had an instinct about that when I read it, I thought, "This is a big one, this one." And that's what happened and it put me back into the mainstream, I suppose, if that's what you want to call it, of the movie industry, but I'm very…what's the word? Objective about it, I think. Someone said, "Now how do you account for your success?" I believe I'm as good as you tell me and I am or as good as my last job. It's all hit or miss, you know, there are no airtight guarantees. I hope this film, for example, works out and it's successful and it gets its story across.

Reba: This is a more personal one. Why, at this point in your career, why would you do stunts that could hurt you? You did it in *The Edge* and then you didn't learn and then you come back and you do it again. What do you think? Is it that big men like to play?

Anthony Hopkins: Yeah, that's what I've always wanted to do. I never wanted to be a stunt man because they're crazy—great respect for stunt people. But it's a lot of fun to barge around with the action just as long as you don't hurt anyone. It's a lot of fun. I actually chased kids around the street playing cowboys and bad guys when I was kid like all children.

Reba: I don't know if you can remember this and I hope you can. In doing the research, one of the things that intrigued me because I don't think the town you came from in Wales was exactly big, but to turn out two major international stars is amazing. You actually met Richard Burton when you were fifteen and that it changed your life. In what way?

Anthony Hopkins: Well, I was pretty stupid in school. I was such a poor student. I went and asked him for his autograph. And he signed my autograph. And I thought, I want to be like that. I want to get out of this place, not out of Wales, but out of the, you know, bleak landscape of my mind. I just want to because I was hopeless to school. I just didn't have a clue. My father and mother worried about me. They thought I was going to end up as a failure, and I didn't want to do it. I wanted to be a musician initially. I just want to be rich and famous. And I tried all things. And so, I became an actor and it took me a long time. But I was very lucky. I fell on my feet. I'm like a cat with nine lives. And from those long experiences over the years, I've had my ups and downs, but it's all been valuable, and I figured out now that my life's none of my business. When I try to make it my business it all falls apart. So, I have a lot of faith in life itself in myself, my inner self, and live moment by moment, live day by day.

Reba: How draining is it to play someone like Ethan, so volatile?

Anthony Hopkins: It's not draining at all. It's a job. It's something I do. I mean, what is draining is if you've gone too long in the day and do fifteen-hour days, and sometimes what is draining is if a director insists on doing take after take after take. That is draining, and that's stupid. That's an exercise in futility. And there are some directors who want to do fifty takes and I don't know why. I can't work like that. So, it's not draining at all. And even in intense scenes, I mean, sure, you don't feel like a million dollars the end of doing an intense scene, but it's not that intense in itself.

Reba: They're going to kill me, but I've got to ask because I'll never get another chance with you. What does fame feel like? You've done it all. Do you wear it with a comfort level? Do you enjoy the fame that you have?

Anthony Hopkins: Oh, yeah, when people come over to me in a restaurant, oh, I get nice chair in the restaurant and the table, people come over and say, "I saw that film." I say, "Thank you very much," and I'm hopefully very gracious and sign an autograph. I do this, spend a bit of time saying hello. You know, it goes the person that comes over and says they like my work. They're the people keeping me in work; they've paid me my salary. And I don't want to sound so corny. You know, Jimmy Stewart episode ever so modest, but you know, the people want to see me and shake hands and congratulating me are people who paid me my salary, keeping me in work.

I understood Hopkins's behavior all too well as I am also an addict, but our vices are very different. In fact, if you didn't know me you would have thought I was an alcoholic, as my behavior was very much like what I experienced with Hopkins when he was so rude to me on that press junket. A complete disregard for another person, place, or thing for as long as it took to get the fix needed. It did not take much for me to also lose it, which I did quite often in the six years I felt I was being held hostage by sugar. I never told him about the *Zorro* interview.

29
JULIA ROBERTS

I kept running into problems with the same publicist who black-balled me. Even though studios wanted me, I wasn't invited to any of the publicist's star's press junkets. I never knew that a personal publicist could prevent me from working so much, as it had never happened to me until then. Studios made their decisions based on money and at that time I had a big following in the sixty countries where my interviews were being placed by each studio's on-site personnel and played by the producers of thousands of television shows who loved my interview style. To the international world of television stations, I was their Hollywood insider.

Once Julia Roberts fired her personal publicist, I was invited to interview her for the international publicity for *Runaway Bride*. I fell in love with Julia Roberts when I saw her in *Pretty Woman*, the film that made her jump off the screen and become a star right before my eyes. That one film changed everything for her.

I had waited a long time to do this interview and was excited. I was not just a journalist, but a fan. I had just interviewed her boyfriend at the time, Benjamin Bratt, for another film and he sent her a video message, which I delivered in a wrapped VHS tape. It was a great way to break the ice in this important first meeting. Lucky for me, I had sat down with Gary Marshall, the director of *Runaway Bride*, first, and he told me that she couldn't leave the bell rope alone, so he put it in the film and I asked a question about it. The *Runaway Bride* interview was filled with lots of interesting moments, so I was able to cut more than one television segment thanks to the advice I got from Andy Kean—try to sell as many slices of your "baloney" interview as possible.

It didn't happen very often, but on this first-time interview with her, there was magic.

Reba: Did you perform around the house growing up?

Julia Roberts: I come from a family of performers, so I guess in an unconscious way we were all always entertaining one another, but I didn't put on plays or shows. I had the occasional flea market dress-up moment where I would put on a Spanish yellow gown and play my ukulele for my dad, I guess that's performing.

Reba: So, when was it that you decided to take acting seriously?

Julia Roberts: I was about seventeen. Did I say the words out loud because again, coming from a family of performers, it's a daunting thing to admit to or confess or whatever it is, so it wasn't really until push came to shove that I said that's what I wanted to pursue.

Reba: Did your mother say you're too young?

Julia Roberts: The thing is, I have a sister who had already moved to New York and was in acting school , so she really paved the way. I had a much smoother transition than she did because for me it was having the same scenario I had had at home my entire life , but in New York because we lived together and I had that security and she was always the anchor to all the madness of life so it was really easy for me.

Reba: Lucky that you weren't the oldest.

Julia Roberts: Yes.

Reba: But I have a feeling that you share more than just your looks with your character. I just got the feeling that you really understood her.

Julia Roberts: It's funny because she was such a puzzle to me. And I think the one thing that we had in common that made me realize that I could work out the rest of it that I didn't understand was her sense of wackiness. Her sense of curiosity of just things. I really enjoyed all that, like the stuff with the bell—all that sort of stuff in the movie is really just me calling myself a different name and so that was the glue that held the rest of it together, all the things that I really struggled to sort out and really struggled to explain through the course of the movie was really facilitated by all the things that I understood.

Reba: I have to pick up on the bell. Was this a fantasy? I have never seen anyone have so much fun pulling on a bell rope and you really did it, didn't you?

Julia Roberts: Yes, I was doing it when we were rehearsing, I was constantly playing with this rope that was just hanging in my face, I'm like a kid and I remember being like eight years old visiting my grandma at this old age home where she lived and had so much fun with all these people, they played cards all the time and they had dances and but in her bathtub there was a string that hung right in front of my face as I sat in the bathtub and she always said, "Now don't pull that string" and of course, by the third bath, I pull the string and there was twelve eighty-year-old people in the bathroom in a flash. And the string to the bell was the same kind of thing and so I played with it and Gary put it in the movie.

Reba: Are you living out your dreams and do you ever say, "Why me?" Do you ever question this lucky path that you are on?

Julia Roberts: I guess it's about gratitude, though. That sometimes I do become so overwhelmed with an appreciation and a gratitude for the blessings of my life that you do, within that, have to say I don't know if it's "why me" but it's to say, "I don't know why it's me, but I'm going with it."

Reba: How do you deal with the fame?

Julia Roberts: First of all, I think the perception of what it's like to be me or just to be famous or whatever it is a lot more daunting than the reality of it. And I think that not only I'm a famous person but I'm also a sister and I'm also good at a dinner party and I'm also a lot of things so, it's just another little tag on a long list of stuff. But I think that everything is a choice, and I think that you can choose to go through it effortlessly or you can choose to have it be a struggle.

Reba: They're giving me a wrap—can I ask one more question about being a tomboy because I think it really paid off in this film? You did all that physical stuff—I think people should know you didn't have a stand-in even for the kickboxing.

Julia Roberts: No, I loved doing that stuff. It was a lot of fun. Gary didn't give me a lot of room to do kickboxing as they hung my bag in a pretty small area and I've got very long legs, so it was a struggle, but I enjoyed it.

After the interview was over, I unhooked my microphone and got on my knees so that my mouth would be close to her ear as I did not want anyone from the studio to hear what I had to say. I then told her that her former publicist had used her name to the studios saying that she personally did not want me to interview her. Roberts was appalled, especially since she didn't even know who I was nor would she keep someone, especially a woman, from getting a job. I'm surprised I did that, but I felt very brave because the interview to me was perfect.

I guess the studio also thought it was perfect. Once we added the approved film clips, I was able to sell them two exclusive programming stories with Julia Roberts from only my ten minutes with her.

I interviewed her again for *Mona Lisa Smile* and brought my daughter to the press junket and when they met Julia stood up, extended her hand, and said, "Hi, I'm Julia," even though we all knew who she was. In 2018, I went to a private screening party for the film *Ben Is Back* given by her agents at Creative Artist Agency, CAA. I ended up spending some private time with her and retold her what her former publicist had done to me. I told her the rest of the story of how I got to sell her to the studio twice and made great money from *Runaway Bride,* and she laughed and hugged me and let me know how pleased she was that she could do that for me. Very few personal publicists were nasty as they all wanted the same thing: the best possible exposure for their client. In fact, that publicist was the only one that refused to approve me to do interviews during my twenty-three-year career.

30
ANGELINA JOLIE

I didn't know what to expect from Angelina Jolie as many beautiful actresses are insecure, have an attitude and are difficult to interview. She had made a name for herself with lots of tabloid coverage with her antics with her brother and with her second husband, Billy Bob Thornton. I wondered who was the real woman behind the crazy tabloid behavior stories.

I was charmed by Jolie as she was warm and bubbly while her makeup was being refreshed. In fact, I wish that had been recorded because a more controlled Angelina Jolie came out when doing the interview for *The Bone Collector*. For this interview she didn't look like she did in the film, as her hair was very blonde and her makeup very pale, but still quite beautiful. I wanted to find out who she truly was.

I opened the interview by asking if she performed around the house as a kid.

Angelina Jolie: I lived with my mom and my brother and he was always having me kinda do little things. Making me show off for him and dress up and do things. My brother always had me performing, and when I got older and went to school, he had me in his videos when he went to USC and he still is the first person to watch my films and I call him and see what he thinks.

Reba: So, would it be fair to say that you wanted to be an actress from a young age?

Angelina Jolie: I always knew I wanted to be an actor. I always wanted to just perform, I always liked just communicating with people. I was always very curious about different sides of life and I wanted to explore them and I wanted to kind of get, express them, and I loved kind of just like doing something and having somebody respond to it and that we have an understanding of that I'm on the right track of understanding things about life.

Reba: What was the best thing about your character?

Angelina Jolie: She was a very complete woman to me. I mean, there are a lot of strong woman who say, "You don't need a man, you don't love a man, or you can't cry and have compassion or kindness." Like me, she is strong; her strength is that she does have instincts and she is emotional and she does care and she is messy and she's soft, but most of all of it's her strength and not being somebody's she's not, she's finding her way through it. I loved her compassion and her humility and her just wanting to mean something. Be useful.

Reba: When you go into an audition, can a director see beyond the cheekbones and lips?

Angelina Jolie: I don't feel very confident about myself sometimes. I don't know what a director sees, it's just I don't feel that way. I don't feel that's what's beautiful is a certain thing, I mean, it's so important— it's never what I want to be or what I want. I have so much I want to say and do and if that's what I'm reaching for—so what I'm saying is I just don't see what I think is beautiful when I see a face and I see things that are almost too perfect? I don't see the life. And it actually gets me angry sometimes when they almost want to change you and make you too perfect, or adjust you to be something that's not human, not normal. But I certainly don't feel that way about myself.

Reba: I mean, this is the way you look.

Angelina Jolie: I have a lot of insecurities. But I mean, I'm very, very insecure, I mean, looks do help in this business and it does but also in this business, I can't believe how critical everybody is of everything and how insecure people are and it's terrible.

Reba: My first reaction to the movie was a movie of faces. You two said so much without saying anything.

Angelina Jolie: No. I think we did. I think I did. I think, I think you, you spend so much time looking into, looking at another person, I mean, he looked at me enough times when we talked about certain scenes and there's scenes where he talks about, you know, what you're worth and you believe in yourself and, and he saw me, and he looked right in my eyes and I stood there and he made my cry—he knew in my life that I had felt certain pains or felt insecure and he, and he saw that and he couldn't hold me and you know, so he had to just with his face and I'm…I'm sure with that moment coming near him, um, you know, you do get a sense of it, it's just another person and it's something else and it's just that, that.

Reba: Does it carry over to you, the human being, when you are able to experience, on such a wonderful level, an acting moment that you want to keep like and treasure it because it was there?

Angelina Jolie: Oh, yeah, I mean that my moments for me are, as far as I'm concerned, they're, they're my life—they're a part of my life, that's why choosing the roles and choosing the films are so important because it's—these are the next, these are going to be the next few months, that's my life and that's the people I was with and the time spent and when you look at somebody when you have scenes with them and you know they're real. Somehow, they're, they're real in their own way when we talk to each other and so yeah.

Reba: Is there any similarity between a detective and being an actor? I thought maybe there was.

Angelina Jolie: There, there is a certain, there's a certain kind of study of human behavior and I think your life is very much, it's, it's very hard to having relationship; you're very much on your own somehow, you're very haunted by, you know, your, your work is very private sometimes and it's, and it's more important, but I think definitely just the study of human behavior is definitely analyzing things and putting yourself in situations—yeah.

Reba: Does anything scare you? After this movie, I don't think anything else scares you.

Angelina Jolie: Like, you know, I mean I would think being, feeling like I was incapable of doing something, feeling useless. Feeling like I wasn't communicating with people, feeling like, you know, like if I had been working doing films and then people did not respond and I wasn't making any sense and I was off track and I didn't, you know, there was no use to my life scares me to feel.

Working on back-to-back films with the same star were my favorite kind of interviews because hopefully the star would remember me and be comfortable. This was the case for Angelina Jolie for *Gone in Sixty Seconds,* which was already in production right on the heels of the release of *The Bone Collector.* This was a two-part interview, one part done in 1999 at 2:00 a.m. on the street corner of Fairfax and Wilshire Boulevard outside of a coffee shop. (A side note, right across street is the new Academy of Motion Pictures Museum where visitors will get to see Oscars up close, personal movie star memorabilia, my video interviews, and everything Hollywood.) The second part of the interview was done a year later in 2000, when the film was ready to be released.

Reba: She's comfortable with all the boys just hanging out doing boys stuff and yet she's capable of love. Is it exciting to play a woman like this?

Angelina Jolie: Yeah, I've been very lucky to find women characters that have, that are strong and are fighting something and they are angry, it's just that they're very passionate about something and that they love men. That's just because I think that just comes from usually any character, even this one was well adjusted a little because a lot of people see that as a weakness, and I think that's a woman strength is how much she loves and how passionate she is. It's a funny thing because I think at some point they would think that they're looking at her sexually and she's the only girl and I decided at some point that she was very sexual, and she enjoyed being all those things and the sound of a car turned her on and everything and it ended being, I think making the boys uncomfortable.

Reba: But are you comfortable playing a character who sometimes gets dirty?

Angelina Jolie: I'm uncomfortable being clean. I'm very...I'm actually...at an award show with lipstick on and my hair up, that feels very strange but yeah, dirty feet and greasy hands and yeah... I mean, I'm doing something just being a big mess. I mean, that's why I wear black all the time. People think it's because it's so cool and mysterious and it's just because I'm a big slob and I spill stuff.

When it came time for the international press junket, she was making the film *Laura Croft,* and to accommodate her film schedule they had the junket in Greece and decided not to spend the money to send me and only sent my questions. This time I wasn't lucky. The guy that asked my questions to both Cage and Jolie set me up to fail. Fortunately, it worked out because Angelina and Nick somehow answered with what I wanted, which really surprised me.

Reba: Do you consider yourself a risk taker?

Angelina Jolie: Yeah, of course I am. It's the only way to live. I've had enough times in my life where I was pretty, you know, we all go through that we're not sure whether we want to go on or not. And so, we figured well, if it's all going to end, I might as well try this and this and this first and then you do all that and you realize you're very happy to be alive because you just woke yourself up and got free, got a little crazy and brave, so yeah...

Reba: What is it that scares you?

Angelina Jolie: Calm. Things that are too staged, too just, you know, I don't like claustrophobic, you know, things that just...if somebody makes me lay down for too long, just stay still or you know, any place you're supposed to be dead quiet, I'll be the first one to crack up laughing. But what really scares me I think anything happening to my husband or my family? You know, I'm more worried about like, I don't want him to get on a plane in a few days. I just don't want him on a plane. But I'll fly anywhere. And I'll jump out of one, but I don't want him near one.

31
AL PACINO

When it comes to Al Pacino, doing research was not a good idea. What I found right before I was set to interview him for *The Recruit* was that he hated doing interviews. I had been handpicked by his personal publicist, Pat Kingsley, to do his only interview. I will not lie. I was very nervous. When I walked into Al Pacino's suite to do the interview, he was already there and I went up and said, "Consider me a gunslinger from the Old West. On my gun belt I collect legends and I am putting you on my belt." He smiled, and I knew he was going to give me a warm, wonderful interview. He didn't disappoint. I had a twofold job: to sell the movie domestically and internationally to sixty countries and 5,000 TV shows, and to sell Al Pacino. The beginning of the interview was all about the movie, and once the piper had been paid, it was all about Al Pacino.

This was not my favorite Al Pacino film, but I was thrilled to finally meet the elusive actor. I wished I could have interviewed him for *The Insider*, which for me was a more interesting film, but he changed his mind after committing to do some promotion. After my interview was over, I turned the two tapes over to Pat Kingsley for her review as she had the right to remove anything from this interview that she did not want to be broadcast. At the time, Pat Kingsley was the most powerful publicist in Hollywood, and for her to ask me to do this interview was a big deal. I learned from Pat that my creating a video profile that humanizes the hype and which was getting ninety percent airplay around the world was the best thing that ever happened to movie marketing. I was very surprised that no one else was doing this type of publicity, but then again, it's not easy to get a star to be really candid when all they want to do is talk about the film.

Reba: I'm sure you're demanding…

Al Pacino: My character is demanding.

Reba: I think you are too.

Al Pacino: Really?

Reba: My feeling is that what I see is a man that prides himself in his craft and demands the best out of himself instead of just coasting.

Al Pacino: Well, I would like to be someone who takes chances and one who feels that I—that's part of the adventure of it, to go into something and not be afraid to screw up. I mean, because then you're reaching for something you must have the freedom, I think you have to have the freedom to screw up, otherwise you run a very tight ship and you get a sort of narrow expression. Your expressiveness is limited because you're censoring yourself. I think there comes a point…that's what's good about working with a guy like Roger because he allows you—he makes you feel free so that you could go out on a limb and take a few chances.

Reba: But my flip-side question to that is are you your harshest critic?

Al Pacino: No. [laughing]

Reba: Or have you mellowed with age?

Al Pacino: Yes, I think what happens is you learn to forgive yourself because it's you in the scheme of things, and you say "I tried." The worst thing they say is not to go for it. But if you go for it and it goes it's out of your hands. It's like that old saying what anyone says about me is really none of my business. So, you hope for the best and a lot of the times things happen, and you have no control over it.

Reba: Let us go back and reminisce. Did you go to the movies a lot?

Al Pacino: That's right. Well, we didn't have a television in the home. And movies were my only connection to the world, really. When I was very little, my mother worked and when she'd come home, she'd take me to the picture shows. I was so enamored with the film that when I'd come home, I'd want to relive the film again, so I'd relive it. I would play all the roles that I saw, and it was a fun thing to do. I should start doing that again. I'm going to relive this interview when I go home. [laughs]

Reba: Did you do it for the applause?

Al Pacino: I don't know that I did it for the applause, although it was nice to get the applause, but I had this ability to mimic coming from early, from early childhood. I would mimic the movies, I would mimic any of the current singers whether it was Al Jolson, or Sinatra, whoever it was and I learned to mimic situations in people just for the fun of it. And people laughed when you did that, so I had an ability to do it and I enjoyed it.

Reba: You weren't afraid?

Al Pacino: Well, that's what happens sometimes to you if you're a shy person, sometimes you hide behind an image that you think somebody has of you, it's almost a pose that you can do and you let your guard down or commit. And it's a way I got into the habit of doing that. I did for a while.

Reba: Yeah, did you like the audition process?

Al Pacino: I'll tell you what I did as a young actor with the audition process because that was something, I sometimes tell younger actors just starting out. I used to use auditions as a way of practicing. Because all I knew was there was an audience who are going to audition you, so it's a good opportunity to work on something. Usually, they'd have a script they wanted me to read, and I'd say I prepared a little something. And I'd play the opening scene in some play or something I had been working on, it would be a soliloquy from one of Shakespeare's plays or one of the great plays, O'Neill or Strindberg, without ever thinking about getting the role. I even tell young actors, don't even think about getting a part because in a way, once you start getting parts, your learning process is going to get less and less anyway because you giving roles, that you are so so-called "right for," quote unquote, which is typecasting, which is a lot of baloney. You're not gonna get a chance to grow and stretch yourself so you're better off sometimes not getting the role, but you could use the audition as a way of trying things out for yourself and seeing if you make an impression on the work you've been doing.

Reba: How did you hold on during the lean times?

Al Pacino: I didn't feel it was tough because I lived in an environment with a lot of people like me. Greenwich Village in the sixties was filled with a lot of different kinds of people who were without money and could live. That isn't the case anymore, it's unfortunate. I wish it was because it's a great city. It's a great place for the young artists and old artists. But the point was you didn't feel poor, because you were dependent, because I was part of a company who took care of each other, it was a communal feeling. You get hungry, sometimes, but then you go find bottles, soda bottles, beer bottles, and cash 'em, in, you get a deposit for the bottles and you get a knish and a lot of mustard, or, sometimes you'd like to get a nice bottle of wine because then you'd forget you were hungry.

Reba: Do you trust that voice within you?

Al Pacino: Most of the time I trust it. It's been wrong, I've been wrong a lot with that voice, too, but that's okay. When you're wrong with your own voice, you can handle it. It's when you don't listen to that voice and you're wrong. So , I would trust the voice in me, but again, always leaving a little room for other people's opinions. To be influenced is good because sometimes we have a tendency, especially when the light is shining on you, you have a tendency not to be able to see as well. My instincts I always felt were better earlier in my life than they are now. It seems as though sometimes I'm a little bit blinded by the attention, so I don't make, I don't make correct assessments. I'm a little bit influenced by the fact that I'm not on the outside looking in. It's good to get on the outside looking in—that's the part of, that's the fun about working because that's when you do get on the outside looking in.

Reba: I read there was a time where you just stayed in character the whole time.

Al Pacino: That was just an awful period in my life, I think. I'm so glad I'm over that. I was doing that because I would be so utterly bored if I didn't. I wouldn't' know what to do. I'd be sitting there and not in character. I would go home so I stayed in character because I felt that was who I was. And that's taxing and it takes a lot of energy to do that and of course as you get older, you don't have the same kind of energy, so what you do is you try to find a way to economize it and staying in character for fifteen hours a day is not the way to preserve one's energy. You have to let it go. So, I have found a good way to work in movies is, if you're fortunate and lucky enough, to have a trailer. You build a little office in there and that's where you do all your stuff: you make your phone calls, you read, you watch a little television, you have a world in there that you can go to between setups and takes and stuff and in there you build a life. Sometimes you invite people over for lunch.

Reba: Looking back, are you surprised how smart you are that you picked the right thing for you?

Al Pacino: I'd say lucky. I'm lucky I did. I'm lucky I picked that. I'm lucky it came to me. I'm lucky I was fortunate enough to have certain things happen in my life. I mean, it's luck. It's really luck. And persisting in a thing. "He who persists in his folly will one day be wise." I haven't gotten wise yet, but I'm, I keep persisting. And I've been lucky. Very lucky.

Reba: You like acting?

Al Pacino: Do I like acting? That's a good question. That really is. Sometimes. Sometimes I do. I love to play in a play sometimes. [laughs] I know that's a funny answer but it's true.

Reba: Thank you so much.

Al Pacino: Thank you, doll. That was wonderful.

Pacino is one of the few performers to have won a competitive Oscar, Emmy, and Tony award, dubbed the Triple Crown of Acting.

When I saw him at *The Irishman* party at CAA, I thanked him for his great interview, which got the Academy to include my interviews for their archive. He responded, "I know, I'm good."

32
JENNIFER ANISTON

Knowing that I was going to use an interview of Jennifer Aniston for the book, I went back and looked at all my interviews from my very first press junket with her. As her popularity built, so did the coverage in the tabloids. After Jennifer and Brad split in 2005, she did four films in a row, which kept her out of the public eye and protected her from the press getting anywhere near her. *Derailed* was the first of her four films to be released and the only one I was offered. The reason I loved this film was that it came out after a year of silence from her, and the news was now all over the world that Brad and Angelina had gotten together. Lucky me, the film was all about infidelity and I couldn't wait to ask "the question," the question the studio didn't want me to ask, but I did.

The interview started on a high note when I walked into the suite and she said how glad she was to see me again. I replied, "Let's get started, Mama is here." There was an advantage to being the oldest person doing interviews as I stuck out for my age—I was seventy when we did *Derailed*. This interview was the best we had done together as she made me feel as though she remembered me and, whether it was true or not, I felt the connection. Let's face it, she's worth two hundred million dollars and it costs nothing to be nice, and she was nice to me in all of our five interviews.

Reba: When did you decide you wanted to be an actress?

Jennifer Aniston: I was very young, and I think it was more like my parents were actors, so I grew up in it. My godfather was an actor. And I love the energy and love the spirit of actors. My dad was on a soap. Still is. I guess when I started doing plays in school, I just loved it.

Reba: Do you still love it?

Jennifer Aniston: I feel like I love it more.

Reba: So, knowing what you know now, did you still make the right choice?

Jennifer Aniston: I would. Absolutely. This is all I want to do. This is all I can do. I love my job. No hassle, no invasion of privacy. None of that would ever stop me from doing that. I could never let them win that way. It's all I can do, really.

Reba: I won't ask you about waitressing.

Jennifer Aniston: I was gonna say, what else am I gonna do, go back to waitressing? I mean, I could.

Reba: The question I wrote was so stupid because I wrote it before I saw the movie, why you would want to do Derailed. But after I saw the movie, you had no choice.

Jennifer Aniston: I had no choice. You're absolutely right. I had no choice. I had a little bit of nerves and stuff. But whenever you feel a little nervous about something and I think you have to go walk toward it. So I did.

Reba: I did not know till the end. And that kills me, because I think I'm smart. So, when you read the script, could you figure it out before you got to the end?

Jennifer Aniston: No, I didn't. I did not figure it out. And I also don't think we should say that because we don't want to tip that there's anything to figure out. Do you know what I mean? When I read this script and like I said, I usually consider myself pretty good and pretty smart that I can figure it out by page thirty. And then you think it's going this direction by forty, and then you think it's going this direction. It just kept going all over the place. It's great. It was very well written.

Reba: Did you ever take a peek at your dark side?

Jennifer Aniston: Have I taken a peek at my dark side? Oh, my God. I am aware of my dark side. Thank God, I don't use it too often. I think we all have to acknowledge that part of us. We don't have to become it totally, but it is a part of our totality.

Reba: Were you surprised—and I'm embarrassed to ask you, but I'm going to ask you. Were you surprised that they asked you to do this film?

Jennifer Aniston: I was absolutely surprised that they asked me to do it. But I was flattered and overwhelmed and thinking this is great. You wait for those directors to come along, like Miguel Arteta, who thinks this is interesting for me. As a director, I'm interested in taking this personality, this so-called persona, and putting that actress into this part that normally would not, you know, would not happen.

Reba: No, it wouldn't go to you because you're the good girl. Not that you're not good now.

Jennifer Aniston: No, I know what you mean.

Reba: Do you ever learn anything from your characters?

Jennifer Aniston: I think you absolutely come out with, you know, unless you're just walking through it with blinders on, paying no attention to anyone, which, there are those actors. I will never forget it, someone said, was talking about another actor, and they were saying to this person, it's not enough to be just interesting, you really have to be interested. That was something that's rung so true. I am so lucky to meet all these different people and sometimes I even learn from their mistakes and have these different experiences and come out a better me.

Reba: Lucinda looks like she has it all. I mean, she really does. So, what was the challenge to bring her to the screen?

Jennifer Aniston: She was, you know what, it's easy when you've got Clive Owen to play opposite, you just play the truth, you play the reality of her reality in that moment. I have waited a really long time to play such a complex character. It was exciting for me to step into her life for a very short time. I loved the challenge.

Reba: I believe this is the twenty-first century Fatal Attraction with more danger. Before, it was just sex and—

Jennifer Aniston: And boiling bunnies.

Reba: Yes. Now, it's sex with the added ingredient of violence. And is this film the answer to infidelity?

Jennifer Aniston: Do you think?

Reba: Yes, I do.

Jennifer Aniston: Have we done it?

Reba: I think this film was going to make people take a second thought.

Jennifer Aniston: I think it will absolutely make people think twice about infidelity. I mean, it is…because you never know. It's Russian Roulette, isn't it? You never know when one's gonna just blow up in your face.

Reba: Thank you for another interesting interview.

Her huge tabloid coverage stayed the same even after her divorce from Brad Pitt. After the interview was over, Aniston told me privately that she didn't love being famous because she didn't love the negativity and judgment that comes along with it. To me and most of her fans, Jennifer Aniston's life looked so glamorous, I never realized how painful it can be to have your life made so public.
Derailed was the last film that I worked on with her and it was

my most successful in terms of airplay. This interview got played everywhere in the world more than once and no one knew I did it except the Aniston, Disney, and me.

I went to a screening and party in 2014 for Jennifer's film *Cake*. This drama dealing with heavy drug use to manage severe chronic pain she did without makeup and with added padding, which made her look heavy. The film garnered her Golden Globe and Screen Actors Guild nominations, and it had been a long time since she had gotten that much notice for acting rather than her private life, which was still tabloid fodder.

I went up to her at the party and told her that this was my farewell tour to say thank you for giving me the interview that everybody in the world played. She told me that the problem with being famous today was that the internet gave faceless people a platform to say anything they wanted. I agreed with her because even I had gotten nasty comments on my YouTube page and I'm not famous. I wanted to take a picture with her and she told me if she took one with me, she would have to take one with everybody, so I said I understood. I was really surprised when, at the end of the party, she came up to me and said, "Let's take that picture."

The star profiles were positioned as the enticement for the viewing audience to enjoy and for local international producers to play. This gave talk show or news producers a programming segment that looked like something that they would produce if they had access to the star. A real interview and not a paid commercial, but it was a paid commercial that looked real.

33

JOHNNY DEPP

Everybody laughed at Disney for wanting to produce a movie based on an attraction in their theme parks, but Disney got the last laugh with over six hundred and fifty million dollars in revenue. I had a lot of fun working on this movie. First of all I liked it. Second, I loved the look and action of it and third I actually enjoyed interviewing the producer Jerry Bruckheimer as his behind-the-scenes stories where sensational. This swashbuckling movie gave Johnny Depp the chance to deliver an ingenious and mesmerizing performance and the world got to meet a very young and beautiful actress Keira Knightley. Johnny Depp's performance as Capt. Jack Sparrow was praised by critics, me and audiences a like. I went into the interview loving the film , but with not too much enthusiasm for Depp as I found him to be a party boy. I knew that he experienced alcoholism and drug addiction for much of his life, and he made headlines with his outrageous behavior not only assaulting a security guard , but also for damaging his room at the Mark hotel, where I did my Meryl Streep interview for Ironweed. I also knew he left home at seventeen, loved music and even taught himself to play the guitar. He got his first break in the film Nightmare on Elm Street. Depp got this acting job when his friend Nick Cage introduced him to his theatrical agent. I must admit that I was very surprised by his demeanor, his answers to the questions and his charm.

Reba: But we're going to do a lot about your career. Nothing about your personal life because that's not where I go.

Johnny Depp: Okay.

Reba: But I want to sell tickets. Wait, I got to say something. I am producing the publicity for the Charlie Chaplin documentary and I pulled a clip of you from the Wonder Years doing the Chaplin dinner scene.

Johnny Depp: Oh wow!

Reba: You had the Diner role scene down because you played it next to Charlie.

Johnny Depp: Oh, yeah. Wow

Reba: Amazing. Okay. Now, we can start.

Johnny Depp: Oh, bless you. That's really cool.

Reba: Sorry, Dizzy will kill me, but you had to hear that.

Johnny Depp: thank you,

Reba: You're welcome.

Johnny Depp: That's really great.

Reba: Okay. When did you decide to perform? And we're not talking about acting, we're talking about music?

Johnny Depp: Yes, I started in a garage band at about the age of twelve.

Reba: And what did you…? You've got to help, come on, let's play. What did you play?

Johnny Depp: I played the guitar. I started playing the guitar. Yeah, probably early in my 12th year and became obsessed. Basically, sort of locked myself in a room for a good year to teach myself and listen to records, pick stuff up off the records. Yeah, just taught myself how to play and so at that moment, it was like, "All right, this is my world. This is my life. This is everything so nothing else mattered at that point to me."

Reba: At twelve, amazing. But you stumbled…I want to use the word stumbled, you stumbled into acting. You stumbled when you give me the answer because I think that's amazing.

Johnny Depp: Well, it was stumbling. I absolutely stumbled into acting, into this career. It was kind of a…I was literally filling out job applications, you know, I was walking down I think was Melrose, filling out job applications when my buddy Nick Cage said, "I think you should meet my agent. I think you should be an actor. I think you might already be an actor and just not know it." So, I went met his agent, and she sent me to read for a casting director. I read, the casting director sent me to read for the filmmaker, the director, Wes Craven, and he cast me. It was impossible, you know.

Reba: What was it like doing that first film? It doesn't matter what the film is, we happen to know but I mean, just the idea of this musically trained kid who did it himself and all of a sudden being in acting.

Johnny Depp: I literally like thought, you know, I can remember calling my family I called my mom and said, hey, you know, I got a job. She said, "Oh yeah, what's that?". Well, I guess I'm going to do a movie, you know? And of course, on the other line, it's "what kind of movie you know?" "No, no, it's not that, you know, it's kind of a horror film or whatever. This thing called Nightmare on Elm Street and they're going to pay me this much," which was like, I had never even seen that much money in my life. And I sort of thought, well, basically what I'll do is I'll do this movie, and then I'll go back to the band and continue playing. So I thought it was a one-off, you know, I never thought I'd end up acting or making movies. Never.

Reba: Was there a time when you actually could say, I'm an actor, and I'm not going to run back to the music because you really haven't run back to the music and you work and you deliver. But can you say it? Can you acknowledge what you've delivered? And are you surprised? Oh, that's the other point.

Johnny Depp: Yeah, there was a moment...I guess it was around just before I did platoon in 1986. That was the moment where I said, I guess I'm going to do this now. I mean, I guess this is the road I'm meant to be on. I guess I'm an actor now, or I guess I'll try to be an actor. And to this day, it's difficult for me to say I'm an actor, you know, I find it strange to say it, because I mean, music was, and is everything to me. So, it's still a little strange. I guess I'm still trying to be an actor.

Reba: But you're not afraid to take on characters that we mortals say are quirky, but when you bring them to the screen, you give them such humanity, that they're really not, you know...Is that deliberate or are you just comfortable in that world?

Johnny Depp: Both. I am comfortable in that world, but I am also fascinated by the idea that this thing that we think of as society or normal society, and what they consider to be weird, or abnormal or freakish or any of those words. I mean, I've known over the years, many people who've been considered outsiders or weirdos or freaks or whatever the word is, and I have, I've found them to be absolutely charming, beautiful, sweet, hypersensitive, hyper-intelligent individuals. And it's what we all consider to be normal society that I find very, very strange.

Reba: How difficult is it to deal with the fame? You are famous for lots of reasons. You were a teen idol. I haven't met a teen idol since I'm older. But how difficult is it to deal with all this stuff? Everybody wants to know everything about you, but you have to live.

Johnny Depp: It was pretty weird. It's pretty strange. It's not something that you ever get used to...And more than that, it's something you hope you never get used to because if you get used to it, you sort of become one of them or zombified or something. So again, like fame is a word that I could never use next to my name. I mean, seems that people in many places know who I am or whatever and that's one thing just because I have a strange job. But I never understood the fascination with the personal life of a person, of a guy who tells lies for a living. I just never got it.

Reba: Okay, but here's the really intimate question. Is there a pirate in you? I think there's a pirate in all of us and I need you to end this interview by giving me your pirate answer.

Johnny Depp: Well, honestly, I agree with you. I think there's a pirate in all of us, and I hope there's a pirate in all of us. We need to have that, We need to have that side of us. The side that pushes the boundaries for more freedom and more adventure and more romance all that stuff.

Reba: Can I just ask one more? Did you do all that swinging and sliding and jumping and…

Johnny Depp: I did some of the stunts but there was a guy named Tony Angelotti, who was my stunt double who's just an absolute dream. This guy was amazing, and he did everything in his power to make me look good. So I got to salute him. He's an amazing guy.

Reba: So are you.

Johnny Depp: Thank you.

Reba: I want to take your look home. I thought you look so gorgeous in that movie.

Johnny Depp: Oh wow.

Reba: I must tell you I want to look just like…Well, without this.

Johnny Depp: Without the beard

Johnny Depp's suite was a two-room affair and after I left the television lite room the adjoining one was a very dark so I was surprised when a hand reached out to me. I could barely see this white-haired man's face, but I heard every word he said. "Johnny really liked you and I replied and how do you know" his answer was "he never told those stories before". I took for granted that he must be his manager or his agent as I knew his publicist, but I was wrong it was his Israeli trained bodyguard who goes everywhere with him even to the premieres. Years later when Depp was starring in the movie Public Enemies there was a big article about Michael Mann the director insisting that the prison scenes be shot at the Joliet, Illinois prison. During the filming the prison historian showed Johnny Depp pictures of his stepfather who had spent time there. I now knew from this interview who was on the other phone line when he called his mother.

Johnny Depp found out recently that fame and fortune does not always bring success now that his career is on a downslide. He is still one of Hollywood's most appealing actors and his fans still follow him and buy tickets for his films.

My Hollywood career came to an end with a bang in July of 2006 when I was fired at a press junket in front of everyone by a woman for whom I had worked for twenty-two years. Teri Meyer fired me as I walked out of the suite after finishing my last interview with Johnny Depp for the film *Pirates of the Caribbean: Dead Man's Chest*. I was flabbergasted as my profiles were getting Buena Vista International, Disney's distribution division, great airplay, and even greater monetary returns. To this day, I still cannot believe that I got fired for asking one extra question, but that was what I was told. Meyer was walked off the Disney lot in the beginning of 2010 and neither one of us have ever had a big Hollywood career again. Nearly a decade later, I ran into Johnny Depp at the Motion Picture Academy screening for his film *Whitey Bulger* and told him that I got fired as I walked out of his door. In telling him what happened he asked if there was anything he could do. I told him I would love a picture. I was so nervous that I couldn't get my phone to work when a photographer stepped up and said she would take it for me. That photograph got packed away along with my memories of twenty-three years doing what I loved.

34
EPILOGUE

Re-watching these interviews from all those years ago has really opened my eyes to what Hollywood was like, to what the studios were willing to let me do, and to how far the stars would let me go. I hope this book does justice to the stars and their stories. Fate had a hand in my career, whether I was aware of it or not. I'm not sure, but maybe it started with coming to LA alone, without money, asking for help, networking, and trying new things that scared me. I really never thought about my early career until I wrote the book *Nearly Famous: Tales from The Hollywood Trenches*, which forced me to recall Peter Hurkos's psychic reading that I would become successful, not famous. As I was getting all these films to work on, I knew I had found my small niche in a big business. When I watched the video interviews for this book, there were a few that had me in the shot, and much to my amazement, I was wearing the ring that the psychic held when he told me about my future. I guess I was slow finding out what kind of career was going to make me successful, and it only took me a decade to get my answer.

When I was doing my local morning talk shows there were no restrictions on any interview that I did with a celebrity, whether it was on a press junket or on my set, but everything changed when I got the opportunity, my big chance, to do interviews for the studios. I have spent this last year looking at my life through these video interviews, which brought back memories I thought were forgotten.

The Hollywood publicity machine was very different thirty-eight years ago; there was no internet, no YouTube, no Facebook, no Twitter, no TikTok and no streaming services. In fact, every film or star story was either seen on your television screen or in your favorite magazines. In today's Hollywood, there's no place for me or my one-on-one interviews as the press junkets usually have several actors in a single interview and the time has been reduced to fewer than five minutes. Most studios only care about connecting on the internet and are looking for a great ninety-second story. I am lucky this footage survived.

When I started, I was given a set of ground rules I had to follow: 1) talk about the film: 2) do not ask personal questions, 3) describe the character and the film, and 4) use a lot of movie footage. I found the rules boring and realized that if I felt bored, so would the audience and, most of all, the local TV producers. I had to figure out a way to make the interviews personal without being intrusive. I had to find ways to talk about the film that intrigued the audience by not giving away too much. My earliest interviews with Jack Lemmon, Jimmy Stewart, Cher, and Chevy Chase were all talk-show-style interviews with few restrictions and little mention of the film as I let the movie footage do the work.

But once I started doing interviews on film sets, I discovered that my time was limited and so was the setting. I could take advantage of the behind-the-scenes footage I was shooting. That footage captured more personal moments with the director and the stars and became a perfect vehicle to promote the film without talking it to death. It took me a while to learn how valuable this B-roll footage was, and a lot of that footage survived. Every film set became a challenge as I struggled to shoot intriguing footage and not get in the director's way and prayed that the stars would be relaxed enough in the midst of shooting their film to talk. I made a lot of mistakes along the way, but by the time I got to the second half of my career, where all my interviews were being done on press junkets with rigid time constraints and studio executives hanging on every word, I finally learned what to do.

My biggest surprise after looking back at all the video interviews was that the interviews I did in the early eighties for the original 120 television stations were no different than the ones I did for the thousands of television shows which played in sixty countries. I realized that the language could change, the story could be different, but the concept of how I packaged these interviews was the same throughout the world. We are more alike than otherwise.

It seems to me that most of the movie stars I had interviewed all wanted the same things. In the beginning it was the fame, the accolades, and the money, and once they got it, they all wanted privacy, which comes with a price by having a publicist provide that privacy. I caught on really fast to how powerful publicists were in Hollywood. For the most part they treated me fairly well and let me do my job (except for the few I talked about).

I never thought that my storage room filled with floor-to-ceiling cardboard boxes would turn into a totally new career. I had kept the videotapes in the hope of donating them to the Motion Picture Academy, which I eventually did. I knew that videotapes disintegrate, and if I didn't hurry up and digitize them they would all disappear. The boxes also held behind-the-scenes footage, stills from a lot of movies, and public domain movie footage.

The first thing I did with the tapes after I stopped working for the studios was find forty-five of my favorite movie stars and had their interviews digitized and reedited. I turned those forty-five stars into "Hollywood Up Close and Personal," my new career of lecturing on cruise ships. I did that for ten years; in fact, I stopped in 2018, and it was wonderful as it took me and my husband all around the world. People were amazed when they saw interviews of Jimmy Stewart, Jack Lemmon, Anne Bancroft, and Whitney Houston, all of whom had passed away years earlier, yet they were as fresh and new as if it was yesterday. That's the magic of video when it survives.

In 2014, my daughter overheard at a party that a company was looking for movie-star interviews. She got in touch with Media Mine and the president Barry Snyder. He watched some of my cruise profiles and liked them enough to meet me at my storage room. He looked at my cardboard boxes and made me a deal to digitize everything. I knew that those cardboard boxes of video tapes buried in that storage room—the ones that did not disintegrate—had a story to tell. One of the surprises that I found was the interview with Harrison Ford from 1977 from the *Star Wars* junket. I interviewed Carrie Fisher and Mark Hamill as well, but unfortunately those tapes did not survive. I guess there was a reason that somewhere in a box was an amazing piece of history.

What I learned from doing the research for this book, by looking at forty-two interviews, was how I did an interview. It was not just asking questions, but responding with facial gestures including smiles, tears, and occasional kisses. Harrison Ford said to me that he had "the best job in the world," but, to be honest, I had the best job in the world.

REBA MERRILL is an Emmy Award winning television producer and Cable Ace nominee. She was an international entertainment journalist whose television interviews appeared in over sixty countries worldwide. She lives in Marina del Ray, California.